# How to
# Get It Together
# When Your Parents
# Are Coming Apart

# How to Get It Together When Your Parents Are Coming Apart

*Arlene Richards*
*and*
*Irene Willis*

**WILLARD PRESS**
**P.O. Box 1254**
**Summit, New Jersey 07901**

**Library of Congress Cataloging in Publication Data**

Richards, Arlene Kramer.
  How to get it together when your parents are coming apart.

  SUMMARY: A guide to help adolescents deal with their parents'
marital problems, their divorce, and its aftermath.
  1.  Divorce—United States—Juvenile literature.  2.  Children of
divorced parents—Juvenile literature.  3.  Problem families—Juvenile
literature.  4.  Adolescent psychology—Juvenile Literature.  [1.  Divorce.  2.  Family problems]  I.  Willis, Irene
II.  Title.
HQ536.R48          301.42'7          76-12746
ISBN 0-9615349-0-7

MANUFACTURED IN THE UNITED STATES OF AMERICA

# WILLARD PRESS
**P.O. Box 1254**
**Summit, New Jersey 07901**

*To*
*Dr. Arnold Richards,*
*who gave us our title*

# Contents

# Acknowledgments

We would like to thank all the young people who were kind enough to allow us to interview them for this book and who have been assured that their confidentiality would be respected. We would also like to thank Joe A. of Gambler's Anonymous; Judge Nanette Dembitz of New York Family Court; Esther Oshiver Fisher, L.L.B., Ed.D.; Mitchell Salem Fisher, L.L.B., Ph.D.; Sheila Greene; Barbara Kaiser, L.L.B.; Irwin Kaiser, M.D., Ph.D., Albert Einstein College of Medicine, New York; the Reverend Dr. Walter Kring; Judith Shuchter Marks, M.S.W.; Tom Mullaney of RENEW; Murray Schwartz, L.L.B., L.L.M.; Charlotte Tejessey Sissman, M.S.W., of the Jewish Child Care Association of New York; Gerda Strika, M.D., Chief of Adolescent Services, Department of Child and Adolescent Psychiatry, St. Luke's Hospital, New York; Donna Johnson Szilagyi, M.S.W., Pediatric Clinic, St. Luke's Hospital, New York; Amy Ward Taylor, M.S.W., Department of

Community Psychiatry, St. Luke's Hospital, New York; Shirley Taylor, M.S.W.; Timmy W. of Al-Anon; Ira Wolfman, Senior Editor of SMASH magazine; the Reverend Paul H. Young, Jr.; and all the students of Rye Neck Alternative School who so generously took the time to read and criticize the manuscript.

A special warm thanks to our editor, Ann McKeown, for her commitment, sensitivity, care and enthusiasm in working with us on the manuscript.

# Preface

About 18 million people under eighteen in the United States have experienced divorce or desertion at least once. Many more go through marital trouble which does not lead to divorce. No, these children have never been married. The marital battles, divorces and desertions they go through are their parents', not their own.

While divorce and desertion are hard on the youngsters who experience them, the arguments, frigid silences and turmoil before the divorce cause even more stress than the final break. Research shows that youngsters are more likely to be referred to guidance clinics before a divorce than after it. Conflict disrupts these children's lives before rather than after their parents' divorce.

Until now, parental marital troubles have been ignored in nonfiction books for children. At the time of this writing *Books in Print* lists only one nonfiction book for children on the topic of divorce. It is for younger children.

*How to Get It Together When Your Parents Are Coming Apart* deals with family troubles before, during and after the divorce. It is addressed to adolescents. Why? Because adolescents are working on specific developmental tasks which make them especially vulnerable to their parents' marital conflicts. Normally, adolescence is a time when youngsters talk less with their parents. In reaction to parental conflict they may withdraw even more. But adolescents *are* able, more than younger children, to comprehend and use impersonal, objective information to resolve problems in their own lives. That is the reason for this book.

We try in this book to help adolescents deal with the effects of their parents' marital troubles on their own lives. We try to help them understand that not all marital conflicts lead to divorce, that the process can be understood at all stages, and that they are not the only ones who have experienced family troubles.

Parents in the midst of failing marriages are, understandably, involved in their own problems. Each asks the children to understand his or her point of view. Children often become pawns in the battle; they feel forced to choose sides. The resulting guilt and conflict leave them feeling both bad and helpless.

Adolescents, even more than younger children, are likely to feel guilty over their parents' marital conflicts. They often imagine they are responsible for the trouble their parents are having. They wonder whether they have said or done anything to cause it. They fear they are being disloyal to one parent if they tell about his or her failings, or disloyal to the other if they do not tell. They fear being abandoned by either or both parents. They worry that they themselves will make the same mess of their own marriages later. Some fear that they will never be able to develop sufficient trust in themselves or their potential mates to even attempt marriage.

Parents want to help their children through the pain and fear of dissolving marriage, but many do not know how to begin. They cannot find a way to talk to their children about the possibility that their marriage will end. This book will help youngsters formulate their questions so that parents can answer them in a direct, personal, meaningful fashion. It is a tool parents and children can use in communicating with each other about a subject they may find too painful to discuss. Talking over conflicts is the first step toward resolving them. Adolescents begin to feel effective when they take this first step.

No book can replace therapy. Because of their inability to ask for help, or because of the depth of their difficulties, or because people around them are too caught up in their own problems to be able to help them, some adolescents do need therapy. The book gives some guidelines about when and how to seek professional help.

This book can be used by friends, therapists, teachers, social workers, judges, divorce lawyers, marriage counselors and clergy. They can give it to adolescents to encourage them to ask questions about the frightening scenes they witness. Asking questions helps to sort out the real from the imaginary. Adolescents can gain control over their lives by separating possible choices from impossible fantasies. The book can help adolescents express the anger, fear and pain they feel. By expressing their feelings, adolescents can avoid overdramatizing or suppressing them. They can incorporate their emotions into the fabric of their daily lives. They can appreciate their own reactions and use them as the basis for future plans.

*How to Get It Together* . . . should help adolescents go beyond the expression of their feelings. It shows them how to use these feelings to resolve their conflicts by negotiating. The ultimate goal of the book is to protect and foster the youngster's image of himself or herself as an effective person.

# Prologue

This book is the result of many talks with people who have in one way or another been associated with marriage trouble, separation, or divorce. If your parents are having marriage trouble, you may feel you are the only person going through so many difficulties. But in these pages you will meet kids who have been through many of the same things. Every person is different and every situation is different. You may not understand or identify with all of the problems here, and you might not like some of the solutions. But by seeing what other kids have gone through and how they have coped with their difficulties, you may get ideas about how to handle your own problems.

If you are in your teens, you are at a rare point in your life: Perhaps for the first time you have the ability to make decisions about how you want your life to go. It is taken for granted that everyone has the right to grow up in a happy family with a mother and a father. If your parents are having marriage trouble, you may feel cheated of this right. But even though you are not the person having marriage trouble, there *are* choices you can make. You do have a part to play. You can get through it more easily if you know several things:

> which parts of a divorce concern you and what you can do about them;
>
> which parts do not concern you and how to stay out of them;
>
> how to find people to talk with and be with when your world is changing;
>
> how to get professional help if you feel more is happening than you can handle alone or can share with friends;
>
> how to turn feelings into energy that moves you forward instead of holding you back;
>
> how to build your own life no matter what your parents or other people do with theirs.

The chapters in this book suggest ways of doing all these things.

Marriage separation is a difficult and painful event for the people close to it. Divorce is a complicated process—but like anything complex, it can be broken down. Certain things tend to happen at different stages of marriage trouble, and there are specific ways of coping with each stage. This book talks about events as they usually occur—marriage trouble

first, then separation or divorce, and finally a new life. The
first part, marriage trouble, is often the most painful. But if
your parents are already separated or divorced, you may want
to read some of the later chapters first, those that talk about
what is happening to you *now*. Then you can read about some
of the things that happened earlier. Many people say that
once something is over they don't want to think about it any
more. But knowing more about it *can* make remembering
less painful

     If you need to find professional help right away for a
specific problem, turn first to the last chapter. It lists many
places you can go to for various kinds of help: from legal aid
to medical care to various kinds of therapy to places where
you can meet other kids in the same predicament.

     No matter how lonely or isolated you feel, *someone* in
the world will want to listen to you and will be able to
understand and help you through difficult times. Some things
you can do for yourself; others you may need help with. In
this book we hope you will discover ways of finding those
people who can share and help, and also learn how to find
help, strength, and action within yourself.

Examples are drawn from the stories of people we have known: patients, students, friends, family, and ourselves. We have, of course, changed names and background details.

# I

# *Marriage Trouble*

# 1

## Making Decisions

The minute he walked into the living room Alan could tell
something was up. His parents sat on opposite sides of the
room. His mother's eyes were puffy, as if she had been
crying. His father hadn't shaved. That wasn't like him, even
on a Sunday morning.

His brother John shuffled in, looking sleepy.

"We want to talk to you both," his mother said. "Sit
down."

John sat stiffly. "Will it take long? I've got a lot of
things to do."

"It's important," she said.

Their father leaned forward. "Your mother and I have
decided to get a divorce."

"You're kidding," John said. He looked at both of them. "You've got to be kidding."

"That's stupid," Alan said. "Who would kid about a thing like that? I tried to tell you a couple of weeks ago, but you wouldn't listen. You said I was crazy."

John ignored him. "What are you talking about?" he asked his parents in a funny, choked voice. "There's nothing wrong with your marriage." Crying openly now, he ran out of the room.

Alan waited till he heard John's bedroom door slam. Then he turned to his parents. "I don't care what you do," he said. "Just leave me out of it."

Alan and John had the same problem. Their parents told them they were divorcing. But the boys handled it in very different ways. Alan recognized what was happening. He didn't want it to happen, so he told his parents that he didn't want any part of it. That's what he meant when he told his parents to leave him out of it. He wished that they would be a happy family for him, but he knew that his parents were not happy together. He settled the conflict by accepting their decision but separating himself from it and from them.

John hated the idea of his parents' splitting up just as much as Alan did. But he chose to act as if it weren't happening. He had refused to see the signs of a break-up before they told him about it. When they told him, it came as a great shock. He refused to accept their decision just as he had refused to see the signs. Part of him felt he could make the divorce not happen by saying there was no reason for it.

When parents have marriage trouble, their kids have strong feelings. This book is about those feelings and how to deal with them. When you have very strong feelings, one way of dealing with them is to find out more about what caused them. Reading this book can be a way of finding out.

How can you tell when your parents are having marriage trouble? Is it any of your business?

For Alan and John the clues had been piling up for a long time. Their mother complained a lot about feeling lonely and about their father not talking to her. They overheard their father criticizing her for flirting with other men at parties. They heard her accuse him of caring more about his job than he did about her. Alan often found his father in the morning asleep on the living room couch. John hadn't noticed that his parents weren't sleeping together any more. He would blot out their troubles by reading or watching TV.

Marriages can have many different kinds of troubles. Some parents have violent, noisy battles. Some parents fight silently by not talking to each other. Other parents hurt each other by doing things that are illegal or self-destructive. Marriage trouble doesn't always lead to a separation or divorce, but often it does. The fear that it might adds to the pain.

Why are kids so afraid of divorce? Divorce is an unknown. But they know it will be a separation and that all separations hurt. They are afraid they will lose one of their parents. They know they will lose some of the warmth and closeness of life in a two-parent family. They know that divorce will bring many changes in their lives, but they aren't sure what those changes will be.

A divorce is only the formal end of a marriage that has been coming to an end for a long time. Any relationship lasts only as long as it meets the needs of the people in it. Keeping up a relationship takes energy. The more pleasure and satisfaction people get out of it, the more energy they are willing to put in. When they feel that the pleasure they are getting isn't worth the energy they are giving, they may complain. They try to get things back in balance. If one person won't cooperate, the other stops putting so much energy into the relationship. So the relationship dies. When the marriage relationship dies, people separate or divorce.

How does someone put energy into a relationship? In marriage it means creating and keeping a sexual relationship that satisfies both partners. It also means saying and doing things that make the partner feel good about himself or herself. It may mean listening to the other person, planning a trip, fixing a special meal, or searching for the perfect gift.

When they have children, married people often feel they should stay together for the kids' sake. Alan and John's father wanted to keep his marriage going so that his sons could have a man around. He wanted to be there as a model of what they could be when they grew up. He thought his boys needed a man to understand them and share their interests.

Alan and John's mother wanted to stay with her sons too. She thought they needed her softness and warmth. She thought the family needed her steadiness and her ability to manage money.

For both parents, staying together for the kids' sake meant being around to give them the special things that only parents could give. They didn't want their sons to go through the pain they believed divorce would bring.

Their mother had heard that children from divorced families have many problems. She had heard other women talk about how hard it was to raise children alone. She was afraid she wouldn't be up to it. She knew there wouldn't be enough money to run two households. She would have to get a full-time job. She worried that if she didn't find work they wouldn't have enough money, and that if she did, her boys would be neglected. She wondered if she ought to stay married so Alan and John wouldn't suffer. Alan and John's father thought they should stay together for the same reasons.

But they decided they had to divorce anyway. By staying together for Alan and John, they were pushing each other farther apart. Each of them felt lonely and misunderstood. Neither of them was really able to give the boys the right kind of care. The gloomy, resentful father hardly ever listened to his sons. He couldn't share their interests or their problems. He was too unhappy. And the mother couldn't be loving and interested when she felt bitter and resentful all the time.

They both cared about their kids so much that they had been willing to give up their own happiness so they could stay together as a family. They had been trying, but it wasn't working out.

Many parents try to stay together for the same reason. When they let their kids know they are making sacrifices for them, the kids feel guilty. Some kids whose parents tell them they have stayed married only for their sake feel they owe their parents so much that they can't leave home to live on their own.

Even when parents don't remind kids of their sacrifice, staying together for this reason can be harmful. When parents are only pretending to be happy together, kids are kept from recognizing and adjusting to the real situation.

In families where one parent is harming kids, the best thing the other parent can do for them is to decide to separate.

A parent can harm kids by beating them, by constantly
tearing them down or by seriously neglecting them. An
alcoholic, violent, drug-addicted, criminal or sexually abu-
sive parent may harm kids. The other parent may decide to
separate to protect them.

Deciding to separate can take a long time. Some parents
think about why they should and decide to try it out. They
separate. Once apart, they feel lonely. They remember the
good things in their marriage. They get back together. Soon
bad things start to happen again. They separate again. Such
separations and reunions are harder to take than clean breaks
because a kid builds up hopes each time. Kids whose parents
get back together think they are finally going to have the kind
of family they have always wanted. When their parents
separate again, they are more disappointed than they would
have been if their hopes hadn't been raised by the short
reunion.

How can you protect yourself from being hurt by this
kind of leaving and getting back together again? It's always
painful. The only choice you have is between feeling hurt at
the time or harming yourself by shutting out your feelings.

Some kids do not let themselves feel the pain when their
parents split up. These kids wind up shutting out a lot more
than their pain. By saying there is nothing wrong, they lose
the chance to do anything about their situation. Other kids
may feel less pain because they have other relationships that
are more important to them. They spend more time with their
friends than with their parents. They may be grateful for the
good care their parents gave them when they were younger.
Having had enough good parenting then, they are able to
be independent now. Still other kids have hobbies and

interests that are so important to them that they don't feel destroyed by their parents' marriage troubles. They can work out some of the anger and pain they feel by working harder at the activities they enjoy. Kids feel less pain when they have ways of separating themselves from their parents' problems.

When marriage trouble gets too bad to live with, parents get out. Some just leave. Some agree to separate. Some divorce.

Some parents want to separate or divorce but are afraid they don't have the money or emotional strength to do it. They think they have no choice other than to run away. Others leave their families because they feel unable to take care of them. They may be ashamed of not earning enough money to support their families. Or they may be ashamed of not being able to keep the house clean or get meals together.

Parents who *can* care for their families don't desert. They can imagine how their families would feel if they just left. They feel strong enough to help their families to separate. They are there to hear their kids' anger and to respond to it. They are willing to explain themselves to their children. These parents try to work out agreements with their partners.

Separation is one way people try to end their marriage troubles. They may have a legal agreement drawn up, called a separation agreement. Legal separation is just like divorce, except that the partners are not free to remarry. Other couples don't bother with a written agreement. They just decide to set up separate households.

The most final kind of agreement is divorce. After divorce both partners are single people and free to remarry. When they have kids, their legal agreement includes arrangements for the care and support of their kids. Their divorce is not just a parting; it is also a set of rules for their relationship in the future.

Divorce is a decision for a couple to make. Although their kids will be affected by it, kids can't decide for their parents. But kids can talk with their parents about how the marriage troubles affect them and about the separation or divorce which may follow. By talking about what they want and how much they want it, kids have more of a chance of getting what they want.

Alan and John's parents decided to divorce rather than just separate because they each wanted a chance to build a new life. They didn't want to just stop living together; they wanted to be free to find new people to love and perhaps marry.

Most people in our culture believe that love and marriage go together. If they no longer love each other, they think they should no longer be married. Many divorce because they want a chance to find someone they *can* love.

When their parents say that they are divorcing because they don't love each other any more kids sometimes become anxious. If their parents have stopped loving each other, will they stop loving their children too? This isn't likely to happen. Most people love themselves, see themselves in their children, and love them, too. They have a link with the future through them. Even those parents too troubled to keep in touch with their children usually love them. The decision to divorce is a decision to break up with the marriage partner, not with the family.

Some people divorce because they have grown apart and developed different interests. But when people have been married long enough to have kids in their teens, they have developed many common interests. They share their kids, their home, furniture and other property, friends and memories. They have grown attached to each other's families. People married this long do not divorce easily. They decide to separate only when they can no longer stand living together.

What will happen to Alan and John after the divorce? Will they be in trouble because their parents have decided to split up? Not necessarily. They may be relieved once the marriage troubles are over. Most kids feel better after a definite decision is made.

Alan and John will not be in trouble because of their parents' divorce if: they don't shut out their feelings; they can understand what is going on; their parents draw up a good legal agreement; and they can stay out of the parts of the divorce that are none of their business.

During a separation or divorce kids feel anxious. Many wish their parents could get back together. Sometimes they get angry at their parents for not being able to keep their marriage together. They think their parents could do it if only they tried harder. They may even have heard other people say this. But often their fear is greater than their anger.

One girl had just come back from her father's wedding. She talked with her brother and sister about their parents' marriage troubles, divorce and remarriages. She told them that at every step she had been afraid that the next step would be the real disaster.

Sure they had troubles and it was terrible to hear them yelling at each other. But she was afraid that if they separated it would be even worse.

Then they separated. She found it was a relief. But she

still felt it was only the calm before the storm. She was afraid that divorce would be the real disaster.

They divorced. They had to sell the house, just as she had been afraid they would. Her aunts disapproved, just as she had known they would. But her father looked happier. Her mother got a job. Both of them seemed interested in their new lives. They weren't nagging her any more.

Next she was sure that the worst thing that could happen was for either of her parents to remarry. Now here she was, arriving home from her father's wedding. Her last fear had been realized. Yet she was actually happy for her father and glad he was settled. She could go back to college knowing that he wouldn't be lonely without her.

Looking back, the girl realized that the hardest part of all was the time of the marriage trouble.

# 2

## Open Warfare

Laura hid her face in the pillow and pulled the blankets over her head so she wouldn't hear the yelling. Downstairs in the kitchen her parents were at it again. The same broken record.

"Where were you till this hour? With some woman, I suppose."

"Gloria, will you cut it out? There is no woman. I was at the office. You're hysterical. Now shut up."

"That's right. Shout a little louder so you can wake the kids. Why don't you try the neighbors too? The Gallaghers haven't heard one of our numbers yet. How about doing it for them?"

"You're a bitch, you know that? A sarcastic bitch."

He was right, Laura thought. She did nag and turn sarcastic at times like this. But he provoked it. Laura wished she could get away from them both and wake up in somebody else's house. A peaceful house. So she could go to school in the morning without dark circles under her eyes. She was tired of putting on an act for the teachers and the other kids when she had been up half the night with her parents' battles. And this wasn't even one of the worst times. The really bad times were when the voices downstairs kept getting louder and angrier until she heard thuds and slaps and her mother sobbing. After nights like that there were often bruises on her mother's arms, and once her left eye was swollen painfully shut. Even then Laura couldn't get her mother to talk about it, and her father was quiet and withdrawn. She remembered how his hand shook as he set down his coffee cup, and how he had left for work without kissing anybody good-bye. She hoped tonight wouldn't turn into one of the worst times.

Laura was going through one of the many battles between her parents during their years of unhappy marriage. She felt ashamed, angry and fearful. It was these feelings that made her hide her head in the pillow and turn away from her friends at school.

She was ashamed of her parents. They didn't live up to her picture of a happy, warm family. They couldn't settle their conflicts quietly between themselves. They lacked self-control. She felt they weren't nice; she thought that nice people didn't scream. Her shame spilled over from them to herself. If she was their daughter, she must have inherited their qualities. Brought up by them, she must have learned their ways. So she must be shameful too.

Many parents battle as Laura's did, making their kids feel ashamed. If your parents battle, you know how she felt.

The best way to get rid of that feeling is to tell your parents about it. By telling them in a quiet, controlled way how you feel about their battles, you can prove to yourself that you are different. You can see that you are not the screamer, not the person out of control; you are a separate, controlled person. By telling them, you also let them know that you care about them and their conflicts. You are separate, yet not uncaring.

She was furious at her mother for nagging all the time. If her mother didn't like waiting around for her father to come home, why didn't she leave him? Why didn't she get herself out of this hopeless situation? It was clear to Laura that the more her mother nagged, the more her father didn't come home on time. Why couldn't her mother see that? She was angry because her mother refused to see the obvious.

She was also angry at her father for not coming home on time. Why didn't he talk about what he didn't like at home instead of running away from it? If he really preferred the company of another woman—or the quiet of an empty office—to his family, why didn't he say so? Why didn't he ever come right out and say how he felt?

Laura's anger at her mother and father was justified. She was angry for two reasons. First, because they fought noisily and deprived her of the sleep she needed to be fresh for school. Second, because their battles were endless and never seemed to resolve anything.

Endless battles which never resolve anything are a destructive way to express anger. The constructive way to express it is to focus on specific issues and to stick with an issue until it is resolved.

Laura didn't need to follow her parents' example. She could have confronted them with her anger the next time they

were together. She could have said something like, "Your
fight last night kept me up. I was tired in school today. Please
keep it down the next time—or at least argue where I don't
have to listen to it."

If you have heard destructive battles between your
parents, you have probably been angry—angry at each of
your parents for the things they did to cause the quarrels, for
the shouting and hollering, and for failing to live up to their
responsibility as parents to provide a stable environment in
which you can grow. And your anger would be justified.
Feeling and recognizing anger is the first step toward using it
to improve a situation. If you keep your anger directed at
specific issues, you may even be able to use it to get your
parents to change some of their behavior toward you. You
can probably never get them to change their behavior toward
each other. They can only do this themselves.

It is up to them to tell each other what makes them angry
and what they really want. They have to come to some
agreement that satisfies both of them by talking it out. None
of that has anything to do with you.

Laura couldn't change her parents' behavior toward
each other. She could only protect herself.

Laura was afraid when she heard her parents battling
because it reminded her of the night she heard the thuds and
crying. During that night she had been afraid her father might
seriously injure or even kill her mother, but she hadn't dared
get out of bed and go downstairs to help. She was afraid that
if she tried, her father might turn his violence against her.
And she was afraid to call the police because her mother had
warned her not to tell anyone outside about family trouble. In
the morning she felt sorry for her mother and ashamed of her

own helplessness in the situation. But fear of rekindling her father's anger or perhaps even turning both her parents against her kept her from saying anything.

If your parents fight physically instead of with words, you may have to deal with that. You are right to be afraid. Any time there is physical violence, someone is in danger. You may have to act quickly and call on outside help. Asking a neighbor to come to your house right away is one thing you could do. Often, the mere presence of an outsider is enough to calm people down and stop their violence. If you belong to a church or synagogue and your pastor or rabbi lives close enough, you could ask him or her to come to your house. As a last resort, you could call the police.

Calling in outside help when your parents are fighting physically may take considerable courage. Often the parent who is being victimized may be the one who told you not to tell anyone about trouble in the family. You may have to risk angering that parent in order to help.

If you don't learn about the fight until the morning after, you might be able to prevent it from happening again. You can try telling your parents how scared you were when you heard loud and angry voices during the night and how you were afraid somebody might really get hurt. If they seem to be listening to you, you can ask them how they suggest you handle the situation the next time. Your question might have a sobering effect on them. If it doesn't, and they tell you to mind your own business, then do just that. Go for help elsewhere. Chapter 14 tells you, among other things, how to call the police and what to say to them. You'll also find advice in that chapter about where to go in case the open warfare in your home becomes too much for you.

Parents' battles may make you ashamed, angry and afraid. All these feelings are normal and appropriate to the situation. If you recognize your feelings and express them to your parents, you will be making life easier for yourself. In other words, it's okay to be angry. But you have to be careful not to use your anger in harmful ways.

There are two harmful things you can do with the anger aroused in you by your parents' battles. The first is to turn it against yourself, and the second is to turn it against other people.

If you turn your own anger against yourself, you are punishing yourself for all the things you heard your parents accuse each other of doing. Laura, for example, might turn her anger against herself by staying home all the time so that she wouldn't be like her father, who stayed out late at night. She might not even realize what she was doing. She might just feel like staying home, or she might not be able to think of anyplace to go.

If you turn your anger against others, you will be making them suffer for what you feel toward your parents. Laura might pick fights in school, punching a girl who notices the dark circles under her eyes and teases her by calling her a "night owl." Or, she might give one of her male teachers a hard time because she's so angry at her father.

Turning anger against yourself or others can do nothing to remove the cause of the anger. Such distorted reactions only blow off steam temporarily. You pay for them in self-hatred and lost friends later. If your parents are the cause of your anger, express it to them directly. That's the only way you can make your anger work for you.

Guilt feelings can mislead you into thinking *you* might

be the cause of your parents' conflicts. Laura was lucky in feeling none of that. She knew that her parents were quarreling over issues important to them—not over anything she could control. Kids who hear their parents arguing over things they say and do often feel guilty. If your parents battle over whether you can use the family car or whether you should have a curfew, you can get hung up thinking you are causing the battle. But you aren't. Part of their responsibility as parents is to handle such decisions without having a battle. If they can't handle them, they may have to pay the consequences by going through the misery of a battle: their battle, their consequences.

When you feel guilty for something that's not really your fault, there is often some truth in it. But you must be careful not to lose sight of one fact. Your behavior is a very small part of the reason they are quarreling.

Suppose, for example, Laura's parents had been quarreling because she got home an hour late from a basketball game on a school night. Suppose she had heard her mother say to her father, "No wonder she has no respect for time. *You* stay out till all hours." Then she might have felt guilty. She might have believed that she was the cause of her parents' battle because they were arguing about her. Maybe you feel this way sometimes when you hear your parents arguing about something you did or want to do. But you don't need to feel guilty. It isn't your fault if they fight. Battling parents will battle anyway.

Feeling guilty about your parents' battling can be caused by something deeper than the idea that you have given them an issue to quarrel over. You may feel guilty because part of you is secretly hoping the battle will lead to a split-up.

Maybe you really dislike one of your parents and part of you would like to get rid of him or her forever. But another part of you says it's wrong to feel that way, and so you feel guilty. Suppose your parents do actually split up. You may feel that the split was your fault because you wished for it. But your wish did not cause their divorce.

On a deeper level yet, your guilt may be leftover from your early childhood. You probably don't remember how you felt when you were three or four. But psychologists have found that children go through an important step in their sexual development at that age.

Little boys wish to grow up and marry Mommy. Girls have the same wish about Daddy. As boys and girls reach age six or seven, they realize this is an impossible dream, set it aside, and go on with the business of growing up.

As you move from childhood to adulthood, your new urge to find a mate of your own stirs up that old wish to have your parent as a mate. Usually this mingling of old feelings with new ones just results in an influence on your choice of boyfriends or girlfriends. For example, you may choose a girl "just like the girl who married dear old Dad" or a boy who is tall and slim like your father.

If you had an especially hard time giving up the wish, you might have trouble with anyone who reminds you of your parent. For that reason, you might choose someone with traits opposite those of your parent.

When your parents battle, it may reawaken some of that old wish that the same-sex parent would go away and leave you with the parent of the opposite sex. Probably your reasonable daytime mind would reject such an idea as silly. You may even think it's nonsense as you read it here. But part of you may be frightened by it. The memory of such a wish, hidden somewhere in your mind, may be causing you to feel guilty whenever you hear your parents quarrel. This may be a real problem for you. Reading this book and knowing that others have felt this way too may help. Just being told that your troubles are not your fault may not be enough. You may want to seek additional help from a therapist. Chapter 14 tells you how to get it.

Even when you don't feel guilty, your parents' battles may make you miserable. Some of this misery may be relieved when you realize that *battles do not necessarily lead to divorce; battles are not unique to your family; some battles can be useful.*

If your parents are battling all the time, you may be afraid they will split up. But battles do not always lead to divorce. Not even a marriage torn by open warfare necessarily ends in divorce.

One or both parents may change. They may get help from a religious counselor or marriage counselor. They may learn from their battles how to make their marriage better for both of them.

Or they may stay together, miserably. In that case, you will have to protect yourself by spending as much time away from them as possible.

If your parents divorce, it could put an end to their battles and provide relief for them and you. You will probably feel your life is better after your parents' divorce. There are some parents, however, who keep on fighting even after their divorce. If your parents do that, you will have to learn how to stay out of it.

If you don't know whether they are going to split up, ask

them. Some parents won't give you a straight answer. But unless you ask, you won't get any answer at all. Asking isn't likely to change their plans, but it may give you information you need to make your own plans.

Yours is not the only family that battles. A family is a coming together of different people with different needs, wishes and personalities. Some of these needs and wishes are going to clash. All families, even happy ones, have conflicts. The difference between unhappy families and others is in how they handle them. Battles are conflicts which have gotten out of control.

To resolve any conflict, the issues must be stated and so must the feelings that go with them. All the parties must agree on what issues should be discussed. Then they need to bargain until they reach an agreement that everyone can live with. But the hardest part of this kind of negotiating is putting up with the anger that gets expressed at the beginning. Other people's anger is hard enough to take; your own anger is often the hardest to take of all.

Maybe your parents, who have always been quiet before, have just started battling openly. The suddenness of this can be frightening. But it could mean their marriage is getting better. They may be finally ready to confront some of the real differences between them. By confronting these differences instead of burying them, they may be working their way through to a warmer, closer relationship. The open battles could be more productive than silent battles they might have been having before.

# 3

## The Silent Battle

Mark finished the last of his meatloaf, sopping up the gravy with a piece of bread. It was good, but he felt guilty. The clock over the kitchen sink said 6:45, and his Mom wasn't due home till seven.

He glanced across the table at his father, who was behind a book, puffing on a cigar and looking satisfied. He always looked that way when it was his turn to cook. Behind him the sink was filled with dirty pots. They should have been filled with hot water and left to soak, but his father showed no sign of getting up to do it. Mark didn't feel much like doing it either. He was achy and sore from football practice and still had about three hours of homework ahead of him tonight—not to mention the work he had to do on the term paper which was due in two days. Besides, the kitchen was steamy and full of cigar smoke and cooking odors, and he wanted to escape to his room.

He was just pushing his chair back when he heard his mother's car pull into the driveway. He sat down again. The chocolate layer cake they had for dessert was still on the table in its cardboard box. He wasn't really hungry anymore, but he helped himself to a piece of cake anyway.

His mother came in and stood in the kitchen doorway. He could see her expression change as she took in the dishes with the remains of dinner on the table, the open bakery carton, the pots in the sink, the cloud of cigar smoke. She set down her briefcase carefully.

"How was your day, Mom?"

"Exhausting. Practice go okay?"

"I may quit the team."

It was a bombshell, but she didn't acknowledge it. She probably hadn't even heard him. She was already busy at the sink.


Mark's family didn't battle openly. No one shouted; no angry words were exchanged. But anger was in the air.

This particular evening was one of many like it. Mark's father prepared their dinner, but prevented his wife from enjoying it with the family by serving it before she got there. Neither parent greeted the other when Mark's mother arrived home. His father left for the front porch without speaking to her. All these were angry acts. They expressed the feelings that Mark's father didn't put into words.

Mark's mother didn't come in like someone who was glad to be there. She didn't say anything nice about the good food smells in the kitchen. She didn't kiss her husband or her son. Instead, she stood in the doorway long enough for her family to notice that she was annoyed. She walked over to the sink as if the dishes were more important than the food or the people. She didn't express her anger in words either.

Because they were so afraid to express their anger to each other, Mark's parents gave up talking to each other. His father buried his feelings in his cigar and book; his mother washed hers down the sink. Both felt isolated. They used Mark to fill their loneliness. His father tried to make Mark his ally by having dinner with him; his mother pulled him to her side by talking to him and not to his father when she came in. Mark felt pulled in two directions.

Their silence made Mark feel edgy and uncomfortable. He couldn't think of what to say to either of them. He had tried to open up with the remark about the football team. After waiting all this time to talk about his troubles on the team, he felt angry and rejected because no one paid any attention to what he said. He couldn't figure out why they were so silent. He wished they would talk to each other like other kids' parents. They didn't seem to care about how he felt or what he needed. Worst of all, they didn't give him the feeling that they were on his side. He felt all alone.

If Mark had heard his parents shouting, he would have realized they were battling. Because their battle was silent, he was confused.

He couldn't see that his father was really angry because his mother's work kept her away from home so many hours at a time. He couldn't see that while his parents took turns cooking dinner they each resented it after a hard day's work. He didn't know that they both felt guilty. His father felt guilty because there was a conflict between his feelings and his sense of fairness. His sense of fairness told him that since they both worked they should share household tasks. His feelings told him he would like to come home after a hard day's work to find dinner on the table.

Mark couldn't see why his mother didn't just say how angry she was about their eating without her. He didn't realize that she also felt guilty. Her sense of fairness told her they should share the tasks, but she still felt her husband was doing her a favor whenever he cooked. She felt she had no right to complain. That was why she couldn't express her anger.

Some parents can't or won't battle openly. Rather than express their anger in words, they show it with their actions. When their behavior includes fighting and yelling, it's very easy to tell it's a battle. But when one parent gets up and walks out of the room when the other comes in, the anger is not so easy to see. The angry person doesn't even have to take responsibility for his anger. He can say something like, "Who's angry? I'm just going out on the porch." When that happens, negotiation is impossible.

When people won't admit they're angry, you have no way of knowing what their anger is about. If you don't know what it's about, you can't change what caused it.

People who won't admit they're angry may be afraid that if they express it, their anger will get out of control and lead to violence. Or, they may be afraid that the other person will become so angry in return that the relationship will be destroyed.

If your parents handle their anger this way, their marriage is in trouble. People who hold their anger in to avoid hurting others often wind up hurting others even more.

People who hold in their anger because they are afraid of losing a relationship are almost certain to lose it anyway because they hold in their anger.

Mark's mother held in her anger; it built up inside her. She could have expressed her anger to her husband, fought for what she wanted and found out what he wanted. That would have brought them closer together. Instead, she told Mark. He felt guilty about talking behind his father's back. He sensed that his mother was pushing him to take sides in a situation that wasn't any of his business. By expressing her anger to Mark instead of to her husband, she was forcing herself and Mark away from him.

When parents are silent, it's hard to figure out what's going on between them. There are angry silences and there are comfortable silences. You can usually feel when silence is comfortable. But when it's uncomfortable, it can get confusing. Are they mad at each other? At you? Maybe they can't stand each other. Some parents carry silence and avoidance so far that they never even seem to see each other. There are many ways they can avoid each other. They may take separate vacations; arrange their work schedule so that they are on different shifts; plan to live far away from where one of them works; or choose completely different ways of spending their free time.

By taking separate vacations, for example, they avoid battling over whether to go to the mountains or to the beach, whether to camp out or visit relatives, whether to look for excitement or rest. They avoid open warfare by carrying on their battle silently. But they lose the chance to negotiate an agreement that would be satisfying to both of them. They miss the chance to reach agreements like half the vacation in each place, or this year one place, next year the other, or an island where the mountains are close to the shore. They miss the closeness that comes from working out an agreement together. They also miss the shared pleasures of the vacation itself.

Arranging to work on different schedules is a way some parents may avoid open battles. Since they spend less time together, there is less time for fighting. But they wind up being strangers to each other.

Sometimes their work schedules leave people no choice about keeping different hours. Sometimes parents must arrange such schedules so there will always be someone home to take care of the young children in the family. Such marriages require extra effort because the partners feel they have too little time together to waste it fighting. So they don't fight. But if they don't express their anger, they will only wind up farther apart than ever.

In many families it isn't the work schedule but the commuting distance from one parent's job that keeps the marriage partners apart. Many families move to the suburbs to get better schools, safer streets, pleasant yards, and neighbors they like. Once they settle down, the father or mother, or both, commute to and from a job in the city. Even a one-hour ride each way means ten hours less each week to spend with the family. Add an occasional bad-weather overnight stay, trips to other cities for conferences, conventions, sales meetings or lectures, and you have a perfect set-up for silent battles.

Choosing completely different activities gives couples another way to avoid battles by avoiding each other. The more they want to avoid battling, the more some couples plan separate activities.

For some wives, spending most of Saturday at the beauty parlor is really a social event. They would rather be there than with their husbands. For some husbands, the pleasure of a Saturday afternoon football game is in being with the boys, not with their wives. This doesn't harm the marriage, as long as the husband and wives share some of their time with each other. Maybe it's mealtimes, or maybe it's just time sitting around and talking. But if a husband and wife spend hardly any time together, they may be either avoiding each other or not caring about their marriage. Either way, the marriage is in trouble.

If your parents are doing things like this, they may be battling silently. So don't be too surprised if they should announce a split-up. If your parents have already decided to divorce or have divorced and the decision seemed sudden to you, think back. They may have been battling silently all along.

Not every silence means a battle. Silence between parents can be just a comfortable way of being together. Or it may be a way of showing respect for each other's privacy. Parents can spend time away from each other and still love each other. Everybody needs some closeness and some distance. Different people need different amounts of each.

What can you do if your parents are battling silently? First, you can tell them how you feel. Mark, for example, could have told his parents he was angry that they weren't listening to him. In many homes, showing anger toward parents is forbidden. But there are ways of expressing strong feelings without being disrespectful. Mark could have said something like, "Listen, I really care about that football team. It matters a lot to me. It really bothers me that nobody's listening."

After you express your anger, you can ask directly to have your needs met. Your parents may be spending so much energy on their silent battle that they may forget you and your needs are there—not because they don't love you, but because they are too distracted. Expressing your anger gets their attention. Once Mark had his parents' attention he could have said, "This thing is so important I need your advice."

If your family is used to battling silently, you are not going to find this kind of negotiation easy. They may find your direct approach startling. They may even refuse to do what you ask. They may be too used to their old ways to be able to change. If after several tries you're still not getting anywhere, go for advice elsewhere.

For example, Mark might have been able to go to the football coach, an uncle or older brother, a close friend or a trusted teacher to talk out his problem. If your parents don't like the decision you reach after talking it over with someone else, you'll be able to remind them that you did ask for their advice.

Like open warfare, the silent battle can be a sign that a marriage is breaking up. Silent battles prevent any talk. People who are trying not to say angry things to each other wind up saying almost nothing. They battle silently because they are afraid that expressing their feelings might lead to open battle. Some of them are afraid that their battles might lead to violence. They don't realize that if they try to hold back their anger it is likely either to come out with explosive force or to drive them farther apart. Being apart most of the time can destroy a marriage.

People who hold in their anger build up a reserve supply. All their old anger stays with them. This is dangerous. The danger is that they will react to a new situation that makes them angry by letting out all this old anger as well.

Parents who battle silently have so much stored-up old anger that they feel they can't express any anger at their marriage partner without exploding. Sometimes it's old anger from the marriage. Sometimes it goes back even further.

A fourteen-year-old boy was playing Monopoly with his mother when his father suddenly got up and stomped out the room. The boy was puzzled. Something had made his father very angry, but he couldn't understand what it was or where it came from. He worried about whether he was coming between his parents.

He knew that his father had a sickly younger brother while he was growing up and had missed getting attention from his own mother. What he didn't know was how angry his father had been during those years and how much energy he had been using all his life to hold it in. As a child he hadn't expressed this anger because he knew how much his brother needed his mother. But now, seeing his wife and son laughing and joking over the gameboard, he felt just as shut out as he had when he was a child. The old, stored-up anger added so much force to his present irritation that it became explosive. Rather than risk blowing up, he stomped out of the room.

In any human relationship, people get angry at each other. In the best marriages the partners express their anger directly to each other about specific issues. They use the energy from their anger to work out agreements that satisfy both of them. If parents can't do this, even trivial matters like leaving the cake in its box on the table or coming home late for dinner can set off battles that destroy their marriage.

Some marriages are destroyed not by how the partners argue but by the serious problem behavior of one or both parents. The next chapter tells about some of the behavior problems that can break up a marriage.

# 4

## Problem Parents

"Hey, this way—quick," Lois said, pulling Barbara away from the building they were passing and toward the street.

"What's the matter?" Barbara asked, jolted out of her thoughts.

"Can't you see?" Lois hissed. "That drunk on the steps behind you. He was staring right at us and muttering. You never know what a guy like that is going to do. One threw a bottle at my brother last week. It just missed him. It smashed all over the sidewalk, right at his feet."

Barbara glanced back. The man in the doorway looked too well-dressed to be sitting slumped on the steps like that. He had on a grey suit just like the one her father had bought last week. Barbara began to feel queasy. The man even looked like her father. She stopped to take a closer look. It *was* her father. In panic, she looked for Lois, who had already moved out into the middle of the street.

There was no way out of it. She would have to get him home. He was her father. She couldn't just leave him there.

Barbara knew there was trouble in her parents' marriage. They had plenty of open battles and silent ones too. But their troubles went deeper than quarrels about who should do the dishes or cold silences after her father came home late. Barbara was worried. Should she tell her mother when she knew her father was out drinking? Should she take him home when she saw him drunk? Or should she cover up for him by taking him to her grandmother's house instead? Barbara's father was an alcoholic. Some marriages break up because of alcoholism.

Marriages break up because of problems with sex, alcohol or other drugs, crime, gambling, violence, or behavior that the other person can't tolerate. Each of these problems can cause marriage trouble. Some families have more than one such problem. As you read about the problems in this chapter, you may recognize some of them. Some of them may have been part of your own parents' marriage troubles.

Marriage trouble may come from sex problems. When a couple can't satisfy each other, they may look for sex outside the marriage, with one person or many. A relationship with an outside partner may be as short as one night or it may last for years. Partners may get together often or just once in a while. But whatever the nature of the relationship, sex outside the marriage always drains time and energy from the marriage.

In our society, marriage is an agreement to have sex

with the marriage partner only. Having sex with anyone outside the marriage is called *adultery*. It is illegal.

Marriage also includes living together, sharing property and raising children. But the sexual agreement is so basic that breaking it is grounds for divorce anywhere in the United States and most of the world.

One boy's father had to go on many business trips. On one trip he met a young woman and had sex with her. They continued to meet. He fell in love with her and asked his wife for a divorce so he could marry her.

One girl and her parents always took their vacations with the family next door. She knew that her father had sex with the mother of the other family. She worried about what would happen if her mother found out. Her mother did know, but didn't do anything about it. Things went on like that for years. The families lived with their marriage troubles instead of ending them by divorce.

Some people believe in open marriage. In an open marriage both partners allow each other to have sex with other people.

Some people think it is all right for the man to have other sex partners, but not for the woman. Others believe sex outside the marriage should be allowed when the partners are in different places or when one of them is ill. Some people think it is all right as long as they don't have to hear about it. Others believe it is all right only if they do hear about it.

Your parents may have an open or partly open marriage. Or one of your parents may be breaking his or her marriage agreement by having other partners his or her spouse doesn't know about or agree to. Your parents' actions may make you ashamed and angry. You may wish they were more like the ideal married couple. You may also be afraid they will break up their marriage. You're right. They *are* more likely to separate or divorce than people who are satisfied to have sex only with each other.

There is not much you can do about it. You can ask them to act like your friends' parents, at least in public. They may agree to this or they may not. You have to accept that they are not what you wished they were. You may decide that you want to run your own life differently. You will have a right to choose for yourself. You don't have to do exactly as they do.

Another kind of sex problem puts a great strain on any marriage. One girl's mother defended the rights of homosexuals. When she was elected an officer of the local chapter of Gay Liberation, everyone knew that she was not just defending the rights of others; she had been defending herself. The girl's father asked for a divorce.

Some parents have homosexual relationships. The father may have sex with another man or series of men. A mother may have another woman as her lover. All people have homosexual wishes sometimes. Everyone can be attracted to a person of his or her own sex. Usually such feelings are softened into friendship or team spirit. They are not expressed through sexual acts. Such feelings are valuable in keeping social groups together. But kids often reject these feelings in themselves. Many kids are afraid that having such feelings means they are "really" homosexual.

Suppose a boy learns that his father is gay. He gets angry because he thinks his father has let him down by not being manly enough. He's afraid that he may become gay, too. A girl who learns that her father is homosexual will also be angry and feel let down. She may be especially angry at his hurting and rejecting her mother. Learning that her father has rejected women as sex partners makes a girl feel less desirable herself.

If the mother is the homosexual parent, her son will feel angry at her for rejecting men. He may get the idea that she is rejecting him. A girl who discovers that her mother is a lesbian feels afraid that she might also become gay. Besides such deep fears, most kids whose parents are homosexual feel afraid that other people will find out and look down on them for their parents' behavior.

Many people believe that homosexuality is immoral and shameful. In many places, homosexual acts are illegal. Some people believe that homosexuality is not the result of choice and therefore cannot be immoral. They believe that homosexuals cannot help being what they are.

It may seem strange that homosexuals ever get to be parents in the first place. But this does happen. Some people realize their sexual nature only after they have been married and have children. Some homosexuals want children so much that they marry in order to have them. Often marriages in which one parent is homosexual are held together mainly for the sake of the children.

Homosexual activity can cause divorce just as any other sexual relationship outside the marriage. It separates the marriage partners, gets them involved with other people, and weakens their bond to each other. The partner and family of the homosexual usually feel uncomfortable about the neighbors knowing and about bringing their own friends home.

If you have a homosexual parent, you need to know that homosexuality is not inherited. You can't catch it. It is usually established before age six, and there are many different causes. Some are physical, some are emotional, and some develop from special kinds of relationships with parents. Usually it takes a combination of several causes to make someone a homosexual. Kids with homosexual parents can become heterosexual; kids with heterosexual parents can become homosexual.

Other people have other kinds of sexual problems. Marriages break up when the two partners can't adjust to each other's sexual needs and don't find any way to change. When this happens, parents usually don't want to talk about it. Then the cause of the divorce seems mysterious. It is often hard to understand why parents who seem to get along are not content with their marriages. If your parents are having marriage trouble and there doesn't seem to be any other reason for it, they are probably having sex trouble.

Many marriages break up because one or both parents misuse alcohol or other drugs. When alcohol or drugs become more important than people, they are misused. The person who misuses them is an addict. While using alcohol or other drugs the person behaves differently. When unable to get the drugs the person may become frantic. In order to get enough money to buy a supply of alcohol or other drugs, some addicts steal, especially from their families. Alcoholics will often say and do things when drunk that they are ashamed of when sober. Some of them are dangerous when they are drunk.

Barbara, the girl at the beginning of this chapter, had a father who misused alcohol. Another girl had a mother who took pills to calm her nerves. The pills relaxed her so much that she stopped doing housework and laundry and planning meals. The girl's father stormed around and threatened to divorce his wife because she wasn't doing her job. The more he stormed, the more pills she took. She became so addicted she couldn't function. The marriage broke up.

The husband or wife of an addict feels helpless. The more he or she tries to help, the more the addict feels somebody is trying to control his or her life; but if the husband or wife accepts the addiction, the addict just gets worse. No addict is happy about being addicted. An addict feels guilty and ashamed. If the marriage partner scolds or nags, the addict feels even worse. To escape from these bad feelings, the addict turns back to alcohol or drugs. Sometimes a marriage can be saved if the addicted partner gets the right kind of help.

One girl's father joined Alcoholics Anonymous to try to control his drinking. The members of this group hold supportive meetings and telephone each other for help when tempted to take a drink. This girl's mother became jealous when her husband went to help other members and when he asked them for help. She couldn't accept his change until she went to another group, called Al-Anon, which counsels the families of alcoholics.

As the addict improves, there are problems for the rest of the family. They are not used to seeing this person sober or off drugs. He or she may seem like a different person. Someone who is giving up an addiction will seem edgy and uncomfortable. The feelings that used to be hidden by drugs come out in the open. Other members of the family have to change too. They have to accept the new strength the reformed addict is showing and not baby him or her. Change is hard for everyone. When one member of the family is changing, the whole family needs help in adjusting to the change.

If your parents are having marriage trouble because one of them is an addict, you probably feel awful. You may wonder if you have done anything to cause it; you may want to help. You need to understand that you have done nothing to cause it. Nothing you have ever done could possibly have made your parent an addict to anything. Addictive personalities are formed early in life. All you can do is to tell your parents how bad you feel and ask them to get help in changing. If they won't help themselves, you will at least know you tried.

If you can't help them, you can help you. You can separate yourself from the trouble. Get out of the house as much as you can. Talk about how you feel to friends you trust. Join a special group for kids whose parents are alcoholics or drug addicts. You can get information about help for yourself and your parents in Chapter 14.

Another threat to a marriage is heavy gambling. Just as an alcoholic needs a drink or an addict needs a drug, a heavy gambler needs to gamble. The parent who gambles uses up money, time and energy. For one boy and his family, life with a father who gambled was like being on a roller coaster. Each win only made the losing times seem worse. Everyone worried about money. The mother, who didn't gamble, resented the father's losing money that could have been saved for family vacations and college expenses for the boy and his sister.

Gambling may set off battles, open or silent. If the family stays together, they are in marriage trouble. If they split up, they may still have money troubles because the gambler will probably be unable to stop. But if they do split up, at least the nongambling parent will be able to keep his or her own money unthreatened. If you are stuck in such a family, you may want to contact a group for kids whose parents are gamblers.

Another less common source of marriage trouble is crime. One girl's father was convicted of receiving stolen goods. All of their relatives told her mother she should get a divorce. They didn't want a criminal in the family. They thought he would be a bad influence on the children. The mother was torn between loyalty to her husband and to her family.

In some states, one partner's having been convicted of a crime is legal grounds for the other partner to get a divorce. If a parent is in prison other members of the family will suffer. Some people stay away from them. The family may be lonely and ashamed. The husband or wife may divorce the criminal partner to get rid of the loneliness and shame. Being apart also makes it hard to keep up the sexual bond that is the core of marriage. Without this bond, it is easier to decide to divorce.

Even if a criminal parent is not caught, there will probably be marriage trouble. The other parent may feel ashamed to be married to a criminal. This parent may not want to be associated with anyone like that. The parent may finally have to choose between moral standards and loyalty to the husband or wife. If your family has this kind of trouble, you'll probably need help in sorting out your feelings and in deciding what you can do.

Another source of marriage trouble is violence. Some parents let out their anger by beating their children, their partner, or both. Often, such people were beaten by their own parents when they were children. They do as they were done to. They can't express their anger in words. They have so much leftover rage inside them that they can't hold it in. Such people can't remain married without using their families as punching bags.

The need for violence can also come out in egging other people on to be violent to each other. In one family, a father who was tired of his sons' constant quarreling forced them to fight it out in the garage. After the boys had beaten each other bloody, they stopped talking to each other for a year. Being beaten or being forced to fight can scar kids for the rest of their lives, emotionally as well as physically.

You owe it to yourself to protect yourself from violence.

If only one parent abuses you, the other may be willing to protect you, even going so far as to leave the violent parent. A decision to split up the family to protect you from the violent parent is sometimes the only way out.

If one parent is beating the other, you may have to call for outside help. This will be hard. If the parent who is being beaten is ashamed and wants to keep it a secret, calling for help will be even harder. One girl caught in such a family sat in her room, afraid to call the police. Her mother was beaten so badly her jaw was broken. The girl never forgave her father. She never forgave herself, either. She would have been better off if she had called the police.

Some marriages are destroyed because one person does things that hardly anybody could stand. One girl's father made loud scenes on the street. If the family went out anywhere together, he would get so angry at the girl's mother that he would yell at her in public. People would stop to stare. The rest of the family felt humiliated. The girl's mother finally asked for a divorce.

Other marriages are destroyed because one partner can't stand things that the other partner does, even though what that partner does might not seem so bad to others. One boy's father refused to bathe or shave on weekends. He wouldn't go out to see people and he wouldn't let people come to the house. All he wanted to do was take naps and watch television. The boy's mother worked all week too. Weekends were the only time she had for social life. Because she couldn't stand her husband's behavior, she asked for a divorce.

Sometimes a marriage breaks up not because of what either person does but because of what one person doesn't do. One girl's mother was tired a lot of the time, uninterested in things, didn't feel like eating and needed a lot of sleep. She was depressed. Her husband tried to get her to look for help with her problem, but she refused. Finally he found her so unpleasant to be with that he asked for a divorce.

Your parents' marriage troubles may lead to separation or divorce if they have conflicts over sexual problems, alcohol or drug addiction, gambling, crime, violence or unacceptable behavior. If your parents are breaking up for one of these reasons, you may feel like the only one this ever happened to. But you are not the only one with parents like this. You may feel sorry for yourself. You may worry about whether you did anything to drive them apart. But parents like this have marriage trouble because they are troubled people. You are not the cause.

Marriages break up for complicated reasons. Your parents have their reasons for battling, whether silently or openly, or for ending their marriage. Whatever their reasons, you will have to make choices about how you will deal with the situation you are in.

# 5

---

# Your Choices

---

*Dear Dr. Richards:*

    *My parents are in a dispute and my dad is accusing my mom of going out with other men. Is it because he is jealous? Will they get a divorce? Should I tell my dad what I know? Explain. Is there anything I can do to help them? Please explain.*

                                  *Worried*

*Dear Worried:*

    *No wonder you're upset. You are afraid that your parents will separate or divorce. You want to do something about it. You don't want them to be so unhappy, and you don't want to lose either of them. Your dad certainly is jealous if he's accusing your mom of going out with other men. But he could be jealous because he's going out with other women and he thinks she's doing the same. He could be jealous because he knows she really is going out with other men. Or he could just be dreaming the whole thing up. In any case, it's none of your business. I don't know what you know, but if it's about your mother I don't think you should tell your dad. If he asks you about her, tell him to ask her. That way, they can deal with the issues between them directly, and you will be able to stay out of it. That's the best way to help them and yourself.*

*No matter what happens then, you won't have anything to feel guilty or ashamed about.*

If your parents are battling, whether silently or openly, you have a right to be confused, even frightened. A lot of things seem to be changing, things that are probably out of your control. And a lot of new problems may be arising that your family has never faced before. Everything seems to be happening at once, and there is no sure way of telling what will happen next.

You need to discover how to live with your parents while they are going through marriage trouble and also how to live with yourself. You have to choose what you want and decide what you're willing to do to get it. You may feel guilty or ashamed. You have to deal with these feelings.

One girl's family had an open battle just before Thanksgiving. Her father yelled at her mother for not having prepared their usual Thanksgiving dinner. Her mother had been too depressed to cook. She said she wanted to go to a restaurant instead. Her father became furious. He announced that he was going to the movies and asked the daughter to go with him. She went, but she felt guilty, both at the movies and at a restaurant dinner later. She felt as if she had taken her mother's place by spending the day alone with her father. She was afraid that she was the one pushing them apart.

Some kids feel responsible for their parents' separation. They feel that if they weren't around, their parents would have to be closer to each other. They feel that just by being there, they push their parents apart. These kids feel that if they weren't there, their parents would have to fight out this battle themselves instead of using their kids as substitutes for one another.

If you have this kind of guilt, one way out of it is to refuse to stay with either parent. This girl could have spent Thanksgiving with relatives or friends. If it would have made her feel better, she could have spent it somewhere alone. Or she could have found a community activity, like a church supper, to go to. You have to decide whether you are liable to feel so guilty choosing between your parents that you'd rather not be with either of them.

Another girl's mother sent her out with her father to keep him from gambling. The mother thought he would be ashamed to gamble in front of his daughter. But the father always managed to take her to places where he could place a bet. She felt unable to do what her mother expected of her and guilty because she couldn't. When her mother finally divorced her father because of his gambling, she felt that if she had only been able to stop him the marriage would not have ended. Many kids feel responsible for stopping their parents from doing things that will break up their marriage. If your parents have problems with alcohol or drug abuse, gambling, violence or crime, you didn't cause them and you can't stop them, so it's no use blaming yourself. You have to resist if the other parent tries to get you involved.

You also have to resist the guilt that comes entirely from within yourself. One boy wanted to go to Canada during the summer. He was hoping his parents would take him. His father didn't want to go, so he and his mother went alone, though not to spite his father. He enjoyed the trip, but felt guilty for keeping his parents apart on their vacation. Later, when they separated, he wondered if their spending that vacation apart had made the difference.

Some kids feel the time a parent spends with them is time taken away from the other parent. They won't allow themselves to enjoy being with one parent because they constantly think of the lonely parent left behind. They don't see that it was their parents' choice rather than theirs that set up the situation. If one of your parents chooses to join you in some activity you both enjoy, you should just enjoy doing it with that parent. You don't have to feel guilty, because you haven't done anything wrong.

One girl's mother had a man over to visit every night after her father went to work. Her mother had been afraid to be alone at night ever since she was a young child. The girl had heard her mother beg her father not to stay on the night shift. Now she knew her mother was doing something wrong. She felt guilty, as if she herself had done something wrong.

A lot of people think that those around a person who does something wrong are likely to do the same. Some people even think the tendency to do wrong is inherited.

If you have a parent who does things that other people consider immoral, you might worry because you've been around that parent so much. You might think you have inherited your parent's faults. You might think that your parent's low moral standards have not given you a chance to develop high moral standards of your own. But you couldn't have inherited your parent's faults. It is possible to learn to act like the people around you, but as long as you know there are other ways to behave, you have a choice.

Kids sometimes try to make up for their parents' actions by being super-good themselves. One girl who felt her parents were immoral joined a very strict religious group. She chose it because it made her promise not to drink, smoke, swear, dance or go to movies.

Some kids try to separate themselves from the faults of their parents by working hard and depriving themselves of fun or comfort. Others are so afraid of copying their parents' faults they try not to be like their parents in any way. Some even seem to punish themselves for their parents' misbehavior.

If your parents act in ways people think are wrong, you may feel guilty. But your parents' actions are theirs, not yours. Any guilt over those actions must be theirs too. Their behavior is not your fault. You can't inherit it. You don't have to copy them. And you don't have to keep proving how different you are. The guilt you may feel if you think you are pushing your parents apart and the guilt you feel because you think you share your parents' faults are both unnecessary.

Some kids realize they are not responsible for their parents' problems. They don't feel guilty about them. But they can't help feeling ashamed. They are afraid of what other people might think.

One girl was ashamed to bring her friends home. Her mother had been sitting alone in the kitchen every day, comforting herself with food and getting fatter all the time. Her father stayed away from home more and more. The more depressed her mother got, the more her father stayed away. The more he stayed away, the more she comforted herself with food. Finally, the girl's father moved out of the house and asked for a divorce. The girl was ashamed of both her parents—ashamed of her mother for letting herself get into that condition and ashamed of her father for not trying to help her mother with what was obviously a serious problem. She was also afraid that anyone who saw her mother would think that she herself would look like that some day.

Many kids think that others judge them by their parents. They think that other kids will not look up to them or want to be with them if they have awful-looking parents. They know kids who are not their real friends might make fun of their parents. This would be like making fun of them.

One boy's parents fought so much that he was ashamed to bring his friends home. He never knew when his parents might start again, and he didn't want his friends to hear their yelling and swearing at each other. He was ashamed of their lack of control.

Another boy hated to have friends sleep over because they might ask why his father wasn't home. He knew that his father had a girlfriend on the other side of town. He knew that was where his father was the nights he wasn't home. He was ashamed of his father for sneaking around and ashamed of his mother for putting up with it.

If your parents look or behave differently from other parents, you may feel ashamed of them. There may not be much you can do besides bringing only your closest friends home. You may find it easier if you prepare these friends first for any unusual appearance or behavior of your parents. Tell your friends what to expect. Then at least they won't be surprised and won't blame you for not protecting them. And being able to talk about it openly is a way of separating yourself from the problem.

There are many ways to deal with guilt and shame about your parents. You may want to talk about your feelings with the parent who behaves in ways that make you feel bad. You may want to talk to the other parent. Or you may prefer to talk to an outsider. The question is which to choose. Try talking to each parent to see whether knowing how you feel can help them to change. Your parents may not be able to change, no matter what you say. If they are unable to change behavior that is hurting you, then it is up to you to find the best ways to cope with their behavior.

If you don't feel comfortable enough to talk to your parents, you can talk it out with someone else first. The person you talk to may help you figure out what's really going on so you can deal with it better. Seeing how that person reacts to what you say can help you judge how your parents will react. Sooner or later, you will have to talk with your parents directly about the behavior that bothers you in order to make peace with yourself. But you may be more ready to face that after you have talked to someone else.

The most helpful person to talk to is often someone who

has a similar problem. You can find out which kids have the same kind of problem by dropping hints or by listening when other kids are talking about their parents. You may want to get in touch with a group of kids who have similar problems. Look in Chapter 14 to find names of organizations that can help.

If you can't talk to a friend or a group of other kids, you might try your guidance counselor at school. You might talk to a minister, priest or rabbi. You don't have to belong to a church or synagogue to do this. Many religious counselors are willing to listen to anyone who needs their help.

Deciding whether to tell about your parents' problems is often difficult. It is even harder when parents have warned their kids not to discuss family problems outside. You may need help in sorting out whom to tell and what to say. Anything you say to a religious counselor or professional therapist should be kept private; it should not be repeated to anyone else. You can ask whether the religious counselor or therapist will agree to keep your visit private before you tell anything your parents might not want known.

What to tell and whom to tell it to can be a serious problem. You may be afraid that every bit of immoral or illegal behavior you tell anyone about might be used against your parent later. Such things can happen. That's why asking the person you confide in to keep your talk private is a good idea.

You might wonder whether to tell one of your parents about what the other is doing. One girl noticed a tape recorder attached to the extension phone in her father's workshop. She overheard her father talking to her mother's friends on the phone, asking questions about her mother's comings and goings. She was worried. Should she tell her mother about the tape recorder? Should she risk getting her father angry? To whom did her loyalty belong? Should she be loyal to her mother, who might be cheating on her father? Should she be loyal to her father, who seemed to be spying on her mother? If she told, she would feel disloyal to her father. If she didn't, she would feel disloyal to her mother. Either way she would feel helpless, drawn into their battles against her will.

The only way out of her problem was to mention at a time when both her parents were there to hear her that she had seen the recording device on the phone. Then it was up to them to explain.

If you find that one parent is spying on the other, you can tell that parent you don't want any part of it.

Suppose one parent asks you to tell on the other. Rather then getting caught in that web, you can talk about it while both parents are there.

You may be afraid you will lose the parent you depend on most. For many kids this is the scariest thing that can happen. But a parent who really cares for you will never stop loving you. Love can't be turned on and off. Parents may threaten not to love you any more. But this is only their way of trying to get you to do what they want. Both parents may get angry at you for exposing what they have been trying hard to cover up. They may both turn on you and tell you to mind your own business. But this is the best thing that can happen because then you are out of it.

You can make a bargain with them. If they don't ask you to tell them about each other's behavior, you won't tell. If one of them asks you about the other, you will tell the other parent you have been asked. You don't need to tattle on anyone; you can feel free of guilt. All you have to do is keep to the agreement you have reached. Your agreement will help protect you from being hurt in their battle.

Minding your own business is such a good deal for you that if they don't tell you to do it, you should ask them to let you do it. If your mother asks you what time your father came home last night, you can say, politely and pleasantly, "Ask him." If she insists on an answer, you can tell her you feel bad about it and ask if you can speak to both of them together. If they will get together and talk about it, you can tell them you don't want to hurt their feelings but that you would like to stay out of their battles.

You have the right to come to an agreement you can live with. If they won't get together to talk about it, you will just have to tell each one separately. Explain that you don't want to lie or tattle but that those are the choices they seem to be giving you. Once they see things from your point of view, most parents will want to help you. They may be relieved to know you are not judging them. They may admire your courage. Each of them may feel they can trust you more than they could if you did give in and tell on them.

On the other hand, telling how you feel may hurt your parents' feelings. They may get angry. The one who asked you to tell may feel that you are not on *his* side; the other one may be angry that you did not cover up for *her*. Even if they get angry at you, it's worth it. You will have saved yourself from an endless stream of demands for more information. You will be true to yourself, so you will feel less pushed around. You will feel more in charge of your own life.

While your parents battle through their marriage troubles, you may be suffering guilt and shame. You can deal with this by admitting to yourself how you feel, getting help from parents, friends and others, and remembering that *you* have done nothing to feel guilty or ashamed about.

A lot of what happens between your parents depends on the problems they brought to their marriage. A lot more depends on how they handle the problems in their marriage. Very little of it depends on you.

Marriages don't usually lead to divorce. Over half of the people who start divorce actions don't go through with them. Lots more people think of starting them but don't get as far as the lawyer's office.

Many things can happen to avert a break-up. Sometimes, the mention of divorce starts a chain reaction. For example, a mother may realize that her drinking is more serious than she had thought. Her shock may cause her to seek help. Her change might not prevent a divorce, but it could eventually bring the family closer together than it was before the divorce was ever mentioned.

Yet many marriages do end in divorce. During the year this book is being written, about a million couples in the United States will get divorced. If your parents' marriage trouble ends in divorce, it will mean changes in your life. The next section of the book will tell you about these changes and how to cope with them.

# II

## During the Divorce

# 6

## Legal Combat

Once parents decide that they can't live together anymore, they have to choose whether to live apart but stay married, to get a legal separation or to get a divorce.

A legal separation means that a husband and wife live apart but are still legally married. Each is free to live as a single person, but neither may remarry. People get legal separations rather than divorces for many reasons. One is that their religion may forbid divorce. Another is that they are not sure they want to end their marriage completely. A third reason is that they may want to use the legal separation as a first step toward divorce. In many states a couple can get a divorce if they can prove they have lived apart for a period of time and have filed separation papers.

A divorce is just like a legal separation, except that the

marriage is completely ended. Both husband and wife are free to remarry after a divorce.

If a couple chooses legal separation or divorce, they must go through a series of steps. First, they must draw up a separation agreement. The agreement spells out the rules a couple will live by after they separate. It tells how they will divide up whatever they now share. If they have no children, they divide their money, their furniture, and any other property they own. They may also agree to share their future earnings. Usually the husband helps support the wife if she has never worked outside the home. These payments are called alimony or maintenance.

When a couple has children under eighteen, they have to agree on many more things. They have to decide who will get custody of their children, who will provide a home for them, and who will support them. Their agreement also includes visitation rights: arrangements for visiting the parent the children do not live with.

Kids usually live with the parent who has custody. If your parents separate or divorce, what will custody mean to you? Your custodial parent will decide all the day-to-day questions, such as whether you stay home from school when you have a sore throat, or whether you should be allowed to stay overnight at a friend's house. The larger decisions, such as whether you should have an operation, or whether you should go to a vocational school or an academic one, are usually decided by both parents. The court holds both parents responsible for the health, safety and general well-being of their children.

If the parents cannot agree on who should raise the children, custody is given to the parent who the judge believes can do the better job. The law says that neither parent has more right to custody than the other. In the past fifty years, however, mothers usually have gotten custody unless there was some special reason for them not to. This was because, traditionally, mothers were supposed to be the ones who stayed home and took care of the children. Now more fathers are beginning to ask for and get custody.

Custody is a responsibility. The parent who has custody is expected to provide a way of life that helps children grow. This means seeing that they have adequate food, clothing, living quarters, schooling, medical treatment and guidance. The custodial parent is expected to protect children from harmful influences. He or she is also expected to help them keep up their relationship with the other parent.

Sometimes neither parent gets complete custody. Parents may get joint custody. This means that they share in decisions about the health, education and general well-being of their children, even though the children may live with just one of them.

Split custody is another way of sharing. When there is more than one child in a family, each parent may get custody of one or more of them. Sometimes the younger children stay with the mother and the older ones with the father. Sometimes the boys go with the father and the girls with the mother.

In some cases custody is divided between the parents. The children may live with each parent for a certain part of the year. While they are living with their mother, she makes the decisions; while they are living with their father, he makes the decisions.

The judge is the one who awards custody. Most often

the judge accepts what the family itself has decided. It's only when the family can't agree that the judge must make the decision.

How does a judge decide who gets custody? How does a judge know which parent will do the better job? The judge thinks about who has the better relationship with each child and a more suitable place for that child to live. One judge said she thinks about which parent has time to be with the children and can teach them right from wrong. She tries to give custody to a parent who is calm, easy to talk to, helpful, good-humored and aware of kids' needs. The judge considers who can help them keep up ties with old friends and with relatives and about who can keep them in their own school.

Sometimes a judge decides that some other relative should have custody. This does not happen often. Usually it happens after a child has been living with that relative for years. Sometimes the court might decide that it is in the child's best interest for a social agency to have custody. Usually this happens only if the parents and the child agree to it.

Most often, the parent who has custody is the one a child lives with. But not always. For example, if a boy of fifteen wanted to live with his father, his parents might agree to let him do that while the mother still had legal custody. But if he wanted to join the Navy when he was seventeen, he could not do it without his mother's permission, even though he was living in his father's house.

Three high school kids in one family told their parents that they wanted to live with whoever got the house. They loved both their parents but they wanted to stay with the other people and activities that were important to them. One boy had a rock group that rehearsed in the family room. The girl had baby-sitting jobs with neighbors. And the youngest boy had just started high school and now had a whole circle of new friends. They convinced their parents to let them stay where they were. Their mother kept the house. Their father rented a cottage nearby and the kids were able to see both parents as often as they liked while carrying on with their own lives.

These kids used some of the same reasoning that a judge would use, only they did it on their own. The judge agreed that the arrangement was reasonable. The things that matter to kids are the same things that a judge uses to decide custody. If your parents can't agree, you may be called to talk to the judge. You can tell the judge what you want and the reasons you want it. There is no guarantee you will get what you want, but what you want will matter when the judge makes the custody decision.

Besides custody, the separation agreement sets up a plan for child support. This part of the agreement tells how much money each parent will give for such things as food, housing, clothing, medical and dental care, education and daily needs.

Child support is separate from alimony. Child support goes on until the child becomes self-supporting, marries or reaches an age set up by law in each state. The agreement can be for a longer period of support than the law requires.

For example, one boy's parents agreed that his father would support him until he was twenty-one or got his bachelor's degree, whichever came first. Another boy's parents both agreed to contribute to his support until he was twenty-one or had finished his schooling, whichever came later. But their agreement also said that his support would stop at age twenty-five, even if he were still in school. That kind of agreement gave him a chance to complete professional school or graduate school, provided he graduated before he turned twenty-five.

Who supports a child? The father is usually responsible; the father is usually the parent earning the most money. The amount of support is usually tied to the parents' ability to pay. It depends on the parents' income and the style of life they have been used to in the past. The support doesn't depend on the parents' feelings about each other or their children. Support is something parents owe kids just for having brought them into the world. But parents have the right to see that their support money is not used for anything illegal or self-destructive.

In the case of the three kids who stayed with the house, the mother got half their father's income as child support. The father couldn't deduct that from his income for taxes, but he could claim the kids as dependents. That worked out best for their family. How much is paid in alimony and how much in child support depends on many things. It has nothing to do with how much a parent loves a child. It has to do with earnings, living expenses and taxes. It is usually figured out by lawyers and accountants.

Visitation is separate from child support and alimony. Visitation rights are parents' rights; they are also children's rights because they give kids the chance for love and closeness with both parents. Good separation agreements have very specific visiting arrangements for young children. Living up to the agreement is easier when the rules are clear.

Many kinds of visiting plans are possible. One kid's parents agreed that he would spend every Sunday afternoon with his father. Another family planned for their daughter, who was living with her father, to spend every Saturday at her mother's house. A boy's parents arranged for him to spend every other weekend at his father's apartment. A girl whose mother moved too far away for weekend visits was to spend every July with her.

The parts of the separation agreement that are important in your future life are custody, child support and visitation rights. Since they are so important to you, you'll want to know what arrangements have been made about them. You might agree with whatever your parents decide. You might be able to think of questions that need to be decided that they haven't thought of, and you might want to suggest changes. If your parents can come to an agreement between themselves or with their lawyers, then you have a chance to give your opinions before their case goes to court.

It's your responsibility to let your parents know what you want in the agreement. You have to tell them straight out. The law doesn't say that you have to do this; the law doesn't even say that you should. But unless you do, your parents have no way of knowing. Some parents ask kids to help make the agreement. Other parents try to protect their kids by keeping them out of the whole divorce process as much as possible. Some parents might get angry at a kid who asked to help in shaping an agreement.

You have to be careful about how you ask. You could say something like, "What's going to happen to me? Who am I going to live with?" The idea is to get what you want and need without insulting your parents. You don't want to make them feel that you don't trust them. You just want to make sure they have all the facts they need, including your wishes, to make a good agreement. It is their agreement, not yours. You are not signing it. You are not a party to it. They are the ones who will have to live up to it. But since it affects your life, the agreement will be easier to live up to if you have something to say about it and if you know what it contains.

What you need to know about the agreement is what it will say about custody, child support and visitation.

You can say which parent you would prefer to live with if you really have a preference, or you can leave the decision up to your parents and the judge. If your parents ask you to choose and you can't choose because you really don't know, you can tell them that. Or you can make a decision based on some practical things. Which parent is going to be living where you want to live? Which one will have enough free time to spend with you? Which parent is more likely to live the way you like to live?

Suppose you do know who you would prefer to live with, but don't want to say so because you're afraid of hurting the other parent's feelings. If you prefer living with your father, you might say something like, "I'd like to try living with Dad." By putting it that way you're not choosing which one is the nicer person or anything like that, but just who you're going to try living with.

You may not have to choose between your parents. If you really want to live with both of them you may be able to arrange things so you can spend equal time with each one.

Suppose you don't want to live with either of them. You might be able to choose to live at boarding school, with relatives, or with family friends. You might even decide to go to one of the colleges that will take you before you finish high school. In each of these cases somebody would still have custody of you as long as you are under eighteen. It might be one or both of your parents; it might be a grandparent or another relative. It might be a social agency.

Child support is another part of the agreement you will want to know about. Who is going to be paying the bills for your food, shelter, clothing and other needs? Will you be living the same way as you do now, or will you have to make do with less? For most families, there is less money after a separation or divorce—not because parents suddenly become stingy but because expenses are greater. Divorces and legal separations cost money. There are lawyers' fees to be paid. And afterward parents must set up separate households. They need two of everything they had one of before: two coffee pots, two toasters, two vacuum cleaners and other household things. They have to pay two rents, two electric and telephone bills. They find that food is more expensive because they must buy in smaller amounts.

If you know about how much money there will be for you, you will find it easier to live up to the agreement. You will be less likely to ask your parents for things they can't afford. You will be able to plan better for your own needs. If you know ahead of time what your clothing allowance is for the year, you won't be as likely to blow the whole thing in one shopping spree.

Besides knowing how much you will have to live on, you will also want to know how long your support will continue. Will it stop when you are eighteen or twenty-one, when you get married, or never? You will want to know whether there will be money for your schooling after high school and if so, how much.

Knowing these things will help you plan your future.

Visiting rights are part of the agreement between your parents. They are bound to it because it is their agreement. For you it is a privilege. Visitation gives you a regularly scheduled chance to see and enjoy being with the parent you aren't living with anymore. The agreement should spell out how often, when and where you will be seeing your parent. It should tell how much advance notice should be given before a visit and how to go about canceling a visit if you can't make it.

All of this may seem too fussy and detailed. But people who have tried living up to visitation agreements have found that it is easier to live up to them when the rules are clear. There is less chance for misunderstanding and hurt feelings.

Even with clear, detailed rules, visits can be changed to fit your other social plans. If you get a chance to help draw up this part of the agreement, you can try to develop a plan that will fit comfortably into your life.

No agreement is forever. Every part of it is open to change. Life conditions change: One parent may get a raise or promotion; one parent may move to another state; or a parent may lose a job. The raise or promotion might lead to an increase in child support. The move might require a change in visiting plans or even custody. The loss of a job might lead to lowering of child support. Many couples go back to their lawyers to change parts of the agreement when situations change. Changes can be made without going back to court. But changes are expensive. Each time a change is made parents have to go back to their lawyers and pay new fees. That's why a carefully worked out agreement is so important.

The separation agreement with everybody getting together on what he or she wants is not the only way to get a divorce. Some couples can't agree. They have to leave it up to a judge to decide what rules they should live by after their divorce. They have a *contested* divorce.

Usually both parties in the contest want a divorce. What they argue about is who should get what after the divorce and what the rules should be. They may argue about who should get custody of the children.

Usually the judge in a contested divorce will want to talk to the children alone. The judge may want to find out who they want to live with. Some judges think that children belong with the parent they feel closer to. Other judges think they belong with the parent who can give them what the judge believes is the best home. The judge already may have decided who should have custody, but may be asking them just to make sure.

What should you do if you are called in by a judge? You'll probably feel afraid. You may have never been in a court before. You may imagine it will be like the trials you have seen on television or in the movies. Actually, the judge will see you in his or her office, called chambers. You will be alone together. All you have to do is talk with the judge. This is your big chance. You can say exactly how you feel and ask for exactly what you want. It doesn't guarantee that you will get it. But at least you will be talking to someone with power to decide, interest in doing what is best for you, and willingness to listen. Talking to the judge does guarantee you the chance to express your wishes directly, and that your point of view will be taken seriously.

If you want advice from a lawyer, you may look in Chapter 14 to find out how you can get it.

While the plans for separation are being made, you may want to learn as much as you can about the plans for you. This may include asking to see the parts of the separation agreement that apply to you. You may want to ask for changes. You may want to ask if you can help plan the parts of the agreement that will affect your life.

These are the facts of separation and divorce. Now for the feelings.

# 7

---

# How Kids Feel

---

"How about staying to watch the fight on TV? We could send out for some pizza and stay right here," Jason's father said.

"But I haven't even begun to study for the math test tomorrow," Jason said. His legs moved him toward the couch. He could practically taste the pizza.

"What's the difference? If you don't know it now, you never will. How about it?"

"I can't flunk this test. I got an incomplete last quarter."

"You won't flunk. All you have to do is think positive. Want to bet on the match?"

Yes, he wanted to bet on the match. And yes, he *wanted*

to stay. He wished his mother were around to order him to study. Right now he wanted her to *make* him study.

"Mom'll have a fit."

"I'll bet she won't care at all. Call her, if it'll make you feel better. Go ahead."

Jason called. There was no answer.

"See?" his father said. "She won't even know. She isn't even home yet herself."

"But what if she calls?" Jason said. "She'll know I'm not there."

"Look," his father said, "I'll make it okay with your mother."

Jason knew why his father wanted him there. He was anxious about the agreement he and Jason's mom were going to sign tomorrow at the lawyer's office. He didn't want to be alone.

"Okay," Jason said. "Let's get the pizza. I can keep calling. She'll be home sooner or later."

He tried calling all evening long. He was worried and angry. Where was she, anyway? Why didn't she stay home if she cared? If *she* didn't care, why should he?

Jason didn't say anything to his father about how he felt. But all through the fight he was uneasy. The pizza sat heavy in his stomach. If only, by some miracle, he could be prepared when he took that exam tomorrow.

At eleven, the fight was over. His father drove him back. "So long," he said. "Say hello to your mother for me and remind her we're supposed to meet tomorrow at ten."

Jason felt abandoned by his mother. He felt as if she didn't care about him. He felt that he needed her to protect him from his tendency to put things off and to take the easy way out. He felt disappointed in his mother. She was the one who usually protected him. He had always relied on her. Now he felt that she expected too much of him. She knew how his father acted. She shouldn't have expected him to resist his father's luring him away from his homework.

He was also angry at his father. It wasn't fair of his father to rely on him for company and emotional support. He was ashamed too. Ashamed that he hadn't found the strength in himself to do his own work. By the time the evening was over, he felt guilty for having wasted it.

Jason's parents' marriage trouble had dragged on for so long and there had been so many meetings with their lawyers that he had become depressed over the whole thing.

During the divorce, all kids feel sad about losing their family closeness. Many kids feel abandoned by the parent who moves out. Sometimes, like Jason, they feel abandoned by both parents.

The feelings stirred up by separation and divorce are painful. The easiest thing is to deny them. "Who, me? Sad? No way!" The trouble with this attitude is that you are forced to deny you have anything to be sad about. "*My* parents fight about custody? *Never*." You can deny all kinds of emotions: sadness, anger, guilt, shame.

People who deny their feelings also lose touch with the events that caused them. The more they lose touch with the reality of events, the less they are able to change anything about their lives. Their energy goes into holding back their feelings instead of into making their lives better. By denying their painful feelings, they are preventing themselves from feeling happy.

One girl started cutting school right after her father moved out. She thought she didn't care about her father's leaving, but her anger at him made her act in a way that was harmful to her. Because she didn't know about her anger, she had no choice over how to express it. If she had recognized it, she might have written her father a nasty letter. She might have complained to her mother. Or she could have told a friend how angry she was. Any of these actions would have helped her feel better. Cutting classes only made her feel worse.

Recognizing painful feelings is very difficult. The most painful feeling is that of being abandoned. Part of feeling abandoned is feeling unprotected. Jason felt unprotected from his own laziness. Other kids wish their parents would make them clean up, go to bed at night, stop stealing, or stop using drugs. If their parents don't stop them, they think it's because their parents don't care. But many parents don't pay much attention to their kids during their separation and divorce only because they are too wrapped up in their own pain.

One man remembered how he felt as a boy at the time of his parents' separation. He stayed with his mother, but he said, "I felt she didn't take care of me. She just didn't take care of me." It was still a painful memory for him.

Kids also feel unprotected because their parents seem less adult. They can tell that the parents feel like children themselves right now. Divorcing people often turn to their own parents for comfort at the time of a divorce. Their parents may not be helpful. One boy heard his grandmother say to his mother, "You shouldn't divorce him. You'll never do as well again.'' She meant that no man as good as the boy's father would ever want to marry the boy's mother. The boy felt sorry for his mother. He also felt that if even *her own mother* thought she was worthless, she could hardly protect him.

Kids often say they feel that too much is expected of them during their parents' separation and divorce. Some parents are not only unable to protect their children; they demand that their children protect them. They may tell them about how badly the other parent is treating them. They may try to get them to listen to their side of the story. This makes kids feel too much is being asked of them. They feel they cannot live up to what the parents expect.

One girl listened to her mother cry and complain about her father's stinginess. She knew there was nothing she could do. She earned some money baby-sitting, but she soon realized that there was no way she could earn enough to really help. She wound up feeling worse about herself because she had been pushed into trying for too much.

Kids at the time of a divorce may feel they are being asked to be more adult than they are. They may try to give their parents the warmth and understanding that they seem to need during the divorce. They may make sacrifices. One girl tried to arrange a surprise birthday party to cheer up her mother. She planned for too many guests and tried to do all the work herself. The party was a disaster. Because she had reached for too much, she ended up feeling worse about herself.

Some kids feel called upon to sacrifice so much that they are resentful. One boy got so tired of staying home from basketball games to take part in family talks about what to do with the pets that he exploded, "I don't care what you do with them. Kill them all."

No one can live through his or her parents' breakup without feeling disappointed in them. Kids feel as if their parents have failed to live up to the ideal they have in their heads of what a family should be—which includes being happy.

A girl whose parents had tried to get back together before they decided to divorce felt her whole world was falling apart when moving vans finally came to take the furniture out of their dream house in the country.

The shock of knowing that the divorce is really happening makes some kids ask: "Why me?" It seems unfair that this should be happening to them.

One boy knew that his friend next-door had a father who was an alcoholic. He knew that his friend across the street had parents who fought all the time. He had always said he was glad he was in his family and not in either of theirs. Then, when his parents suddenly split up, he had an especially strong feeling of "Why me?"

Some kids feel that the divorce proves that one of their parents is not any good. Some feel let down by one of their parents.

One boy had always looked up to his father. When he learned that his father was lying to his mother about how much money he had so that he could give less for his son's support, the boy lost all respect for him. He had always been proud of being like his father. Now he didn't want to be like him any more. He didn't feel so good about himself any more either.

One girl's father left her mother to marry a more attractive woman. The girl felt her mother had let her down by failing to keep herself pretty. She had always been told she looked just like her mother. Now she wished she didn't.

Being disappointed in divorcing parents can make kids feel disappointed in themselves. Many kids worry about whether anyone will ever be able to love them enough to want to marry them. If their parents are going through a divorce, they may begin to worry about this a lot more.

Some kids are ashamed that their parents are getting a divorce. They don't want anyone to know about it. They are ashamed to talk about what is going on. Some of them are afraid that their friends will pity them. They feel there is something wrong with them. They feel damaged. They think that being in the process of divorce is a shameful thing for their family, something that makes them different from other families and that should be hidden. If friends learn of the divorce and pity them, they think they will be damaged even more.

One boy thought that if no one knew about it, it wasn't permanent. As long as they kept it within the family, there was still a chance that it wouldn't happen. He thought that once other people knew, his parents could never change their minds. He thought they would be ashamed to tell other people they had changed their minds and that they would have to go through with the divorce in order to avoid losing face.

By telling kids their side of the story, parents make them feel guilty and disloyal. It doesn't feel right to be listening to bad things about one parent when that parent isn't there.

Even a fight between them would feel better. At least they would both be there to defend themselves.

One girl heard so many stories from her mother about her father's other women that she was afraid to bring her girlfriends to her father's house. She even felt uneasy around her father. She couldn't tell him why she wasn't bringing her friends. After a while, not talking to him about that became so important she could hardly talk to him about anything.

Some kids believe that anything bad that happens to them must be what they deserve. They feel either that they caused the divorce by their own thoughts or actions or that they are being punished for these thoughts and actions. They may not have done anything worse than other kids, but they think they must have for something this bad to be happening to them.

A girl who had to keep house for her father after her mother moved out found she couldn't eat anything she cooked. Although she didn't know it, she felt that if she did manage okay she might prevent her parents from getting back together. Then she would feel that the divorce was her fault.

During a divorce each member of the family feels lonely. Each is afraid of remaining lonely forever.

All separations remind people of earlier separations. Each new separation is painful in itself and brings back the pain of the old separations. One girl whose parents were divorcing said, "The worst part of it is that I moved so much when I was little." For her the new separation brought back all her old pain.

All of these feelings are reactions to the divorce. Sometimes the unhappy feelings become so strong that they shut out the good parts of life. When they last so long that they get in the way of new beginnings and new relationships, the person suffering from them is depressed.

A boy's friends noticed that he hadn't tried out for the baseball team that year. When they called him up to do things with them he always said he was too tired or didn't feel like it. He sat around feeling sad, lonely and empty. He slept a lot. His friends worried about him. They knew something was wrong.

Both this boy and the girl who couldn't eat had symptoms of *depression*. Depressed people lose interest in the world around them. They get less fun out of life. They lose their drive and may seem lazy. Some depressed people lose their appetites. Others fill themselves with food. Many can't sleep: They have trouble falling asleep at night or they wake too early in the morning. Still others always feel they need a nap.

Most people who feel down at the time of a divorce are not seriously depressed. They can help themselves. They can learn ways of coping with the painful feelings during a divorce.

Others feel they can't cope. They need help in getting themselves back into life again. If you are depressed because of a separation or divorce, you can get help. Chapter 14 will tell you how and where to get it.

Not all the feelings kids have about their parents' divorce are painful ones. Some kids are surprised to find that they feel relieved. Kids who experience much pain while their parents are having marriage troubles are usually glad to have the whole thing over with.

One boy went on a summer trip after his parents decided to divorce. He waved goodbye to his old house and said goodbye to his friends. He knew that by the time he got back the house would be sold and his room would be ready in the new apartment he was to share with his mother. The bad times would be over.

Knowing that divorce does bring an end to at least some of the battles can give you the courage to get through the bad times.

Your own feelings during the divorce are not the only ones you will have to deal with. You will also have to deal with your parents' feelings during the divorce. Knowing how your parents feel may help you cope with them.

# 8

# How Parents Feel

David looked around at the job he had done on the garage. It looked great. Clothes arranged on racks, sized and ready to try on. A mirror behind a screen for a fitting room. Necklaces, ties, belts and pocketbooks hanging from the ceiling the way he had seen them in the Provincetown shops last summer. Hardly your usual garage sale. Everything from the photo-offset posters to the flyers to the trays of hand-painted model soldiers was a bit more elegant than anyone would expect. It would knock people's eyes out when they started arriving tomorrow morning.

He went inside to the kitchen to get a Coke out of the refrigerator, then out to the porch to drink it and stare at fireflies. From across the road he heard laughter and the clink of glasses. That's where his parents were. At the Schwartzes' house for a farewell drink. A toast to their divorce and to their new lives. A few congratulatory pats on the back about how smart they were for waiting till he was ready for college. But David knew the real reason they had taken off the minute the job was done. They couldn't stand seeing all the layers of the family's life together spread out for sale in the garage.

He wondered at his own toughness. How come he could take it when they couldn't? Then he thought of college and of the people he'd meet and of how much he wanted to go. He needed to get rid of all the reminders of their old life before he could begin living his own. But his parents didn't feel that way. For them this wasn't just a beginning. For them it felt like death.

During a divorce the whole family is filled with angry and bitter feelings. Some of your own feelings will be caused by how your parents feel. Others will be made stronger by how your parents feel. It is important to know what is going on with your parents' emotions so that you can understand your own.

Separating parents feel sadness at losing each other. They are also sad because they are no longer part of a couple. They may feel lonely. For some, the sadness is just a small part of how they feel. They may be happy because the divorce frees them for a new marriage. They might even have divorced because they wanted to be married to somebody else. But the one who didn't want the divorce feels only sadness and anger. Even when both partners wanted the divorce, both feel sad.

Separating parents also feel angry. They are angry at each other. Each feels the other could have tried harder to save the marriage. Each feels the other could have changed if he or she really wanted to.

One boy's father took a job overseas. It was a job he had always wanted. The boy's mother, who was tired of moving from place to place, refused to go with her husband or to move the family. After living separately for a while, this boy's parents got a divorce. They were angry at each other because each thought the other should have given up what he or she wanted in order to keep the family together. He thought she could have moved; she thought he could have refused the new job. He felt that her refusing to move meant that where she lived was more important to her than whether she lived with him. She felt that his taking the new job despite her feelings meant that his work was more important to him than his family.

People who are getting separations or divorces are angry because their partners won't change. They are also angry at the demand that *they* change.

Sometimes one partner can't adjust. One girl's mother divorced her husband after he was paralyzed in an auto accident. She couldn't stand having him dependent on her. She couldn't stand his constant complaining and blaming her for his helplessness. He might have been able to change the complaining and blaming. But he couldn't change the fact of his dependency. He was angry all the time. He was angry at his helplessness and at her being unable to stand it.

Divorcing people get angry at each other when they blame each other for the situation they are in. One boy's mother was furious at her husband when she had to put their house up for sale because they needed the money in order to be able to live separately. She loved the house. She didn't want to move into an apartment. It seemed to her it was her husband's fault that she had to lose the house. Her husband was also angry. He had put years of work into fixing up the house and he loved his garden. He felt it was his wife's fault that he had to lose all this.

Yet both agreed that they couldn't stand living together any longer. They had to separate. Even knowing why they had to divorce doesn't stop people from feeling sad and angry when it happens. They also feel guilty and ashamed. Some people feel guilty about not having worked harder at their marriage. No matter how much they have done they feel they could have done more.

One girl's mother was in a mental hospital. The girl's father felt guilty when he had to give up hope that his wife would ever get better. He had spent all the money he could possibly afford on her treatment. When he gave up hope, he still felt that if only he had been able to afford more and better treatment for her she might have recovered.

Many people feel guilty at what they think they may be doing to their partners. One boy's father divorced his wife because she was an alcoholic who refused to get help. He felt guilty because he was afraid the divorce would make her drink more heavily. Yet he had to save himself and his son.

Some people don't know that a troubled marriage may be more harmful for kids than a divorce or separation. These people may try to stay together for their kid's sake. When they decide to separate or divorce they may feel guilty because they think they are harming their kids.

Often divorcing parents feel guilty because they think they have disappointed their own parents. Their parents felt satisfied with the job they had done in raising them when they saw them married and with children of their own. The break-up of their children's marriages makes them feel like failures. The grandparents blame themselves for the broken marriages of their children. They think there is something wrong with their children if they can't stay married. If there is something wrong with their children, they think it must be their fault.

Some people may feel embarrassed or disgraced by a divorce in their family. One girl's grandmother told the girl's mother that she wouldn't be able to hold her head up in the neighborhood after the divorce. She had always bragged to her neighbors about her daughter's wonderful marriage and family. The girl's mother felt guilty at taking away her own mother's main pleasure in life: her pride in her family.

Those people whose religion forbids divorce feel extra guilt. They have done something that goes against all their early training. They face losing some of the comforts in their religion. Their families are likely to disapprove very strong-ly. One boy's grandmother refused to speak to his mother because she had asked her husband for a divorce.

Parents who see their separation as their failure at mar-riage will feel ashamed as well as guilty. One boy's mother felt so ashamed at not having been able to stay married to his father that she moved to a place where no one would know her.

Parents who don't want to divorce but have to agree to it may also feel ashamed. They feel ashamed because they have been rejected. One girl's father felt so worthless when his wife left him for another man that he sent his daughter to boarding school and moved to another city. He didn't want anyone to know he had ever been married.

Parents who are separating often feel sad, angry, guilty

or ashamed. Some feel all of these emotions; everyone feels at least one of them. Parents who themselves were children in divorcing families may feel the pain even more because this loss is a reminder of their earlier loss.

One boy's mother had been part of a back-and-forth family. Her parents had split up and gotten back together many times over the years. She wanted so much to be part of a family that she married when she was seventeen. Although her marriage was a troubled one, she stayed with it for many years because she was afraid of hurting her son as she had been hurt. She was also afraid of being on her own. When she and the boy's father finally divorced, she felt lost and abandoned as she had when she was a child.

Some parents whose own parents were divorced feel that they are doomed to divorce also. They may rush into divorce feeling relieved that what they were afraid of has finally happened.

People getting divorced may be afraid of loneliness. Since much social life among adults is planned for couples, the unmarried adult has a hard time. This is more likely to be true in the suburbs and in small towns than in big cities.

Separation can lead to loneliness and depression. Just as kids can get depressed when they are separated from one or both parents, parents can get depressed when they separate from each other.

One girl was frightened by her mother's weight loss during the divorce. Her mother seemed to be living on coffee and cigarettes. The girl never saw her mother eat a complete meal. She noticed the light on in her mother's room all hours of the night. She was right to be worried about her mother's health. Her mother was depressed. She needed professional help.

What does all this have to do with you? It has to do with you because it will affect your life. How your parents feel affects how you feel. If they are sad, it may be hard for you to feel happy. If they are angry, they may take it out on you even if they don't mean to. If they feel ashamed or guilty, they may avoid other people. During the divorce the house may be very gloomy. You may not feel like bringing your friends home. If one of your parents seems depressed, you might want to suggest that he or she get professional help.

Many kids find that their separating parents are oversensitive at this time to everything they say and do. One boy had his bike stolen when he didn't lock it properly. His father was convinced that the boy had forgotten to lock his bike because he was so upset about his parents' divorce. He yelled at the boy's mother. She was the one who wanted the divorce. "You see what you're doing? You're ruining the kids." This father overlooked the fact that fourteen-year-old boys often forget to lock their bikes, whether their parents are divorced or not.

Parents have less time and energy for their kids during a divorce. They are wrapped up in their own strong feelings. Because of this it takes much more energy for them to get through all the details connected with the divorce and the setting up of two separate households. At such a time kids may feel abandoned by both parents. The parent who leaves isn't there. The parent who stays isn't fully there either.

As soon as the divorce becomes final some people feel better. One mother left the courtroom on the day of her divorce feeling "like a kite cut loose from its string." She had finally gotten rid of the tension that came from her marriage trouble. Her daughter was shocked. How could her mother be happy when she had failed? The girl didn't know that the mother didn't feel like a failure. Her mother felt like a success. She had finally succeeded in doing something that many people in troubled marriages are unable to do. She had not denied her feelings. She had faced her problems, she had tried to solve them, and finally had chosen divorce as the best solution for herself and her children.

Your parents' feelings are one of the things you will have to cope with during the divorce. You may find that your parents get angry easily, cry a lot, and jump on you for every little thing. If you understand how they feel, you won't take it personally. You'll get through it.

# 9

# Getting Through It

Carol burst into her mother's dark bedroom. She groped her way over to the bed, wishing she could open the blinds to let in some late afternoon sunlight. When *she* had a cold, she always felt better if she could look out the window. But her mother liked the room dark.

"Mom, here's the permission slip. All you have to do is sign it and give me a check for ninety dollars and I can go on the ski trip."

Her mother groaned. "All she wants is ski trips. Doesn't even ask me how I feel."

"I'm sorry," Carol said. "How's your cold? I would've asked but I have to hurry. If I don't get my reservation in right away, there'll be no more room."

"No," her mother said.

"No what?"

"No trip. I can't afford it."

"But I don't understand," Carol said. "All the other kids are going. It's just like last year. It only costs ninety dollars."

"That's ninety dollars more than I have." Her mother looked worried, as she always did when she talked about money. "I can't help it if your father is only giving me enough for food and rent. I have to squeeze everything else for both of us out of my salary."

"That doesn't make sense," Carol answered. "He has plenty of money. He earns three times as much as you do. Why don't you ask him for more?"

"I can't stand any more fighting," her mother said. "I just want to get out of the marriage. If you want ninety dollars, go ask him yourself."

"Why me? You're supposed to figure out how much money we need."

"I don't want the money. You do."

"That's not fair to me," Carol yelled. "You can do without alimony if you want to. But it's not fair to bargain away *my* right to be supported."

Carol's mother didn't express her anger, so she couldn't fight for what she wanted. She gave up her rights and Carol's money just to keep out of a fight. She paid a very high price for not expressing her anger. She would have to continue paying that high price during all the years after the divorce unless she could let herself get angry enough to go back to her lawyer and get him to fight for a reasonable agreement. Carol's anger forced her mother to deal with the situation. She had to do something. She couldn't get out of a fight any more. If she didn't fight with her husband for more child support, she would have to fight with her daughter. She chose to fight for more child support. In this case Carol's anger provided the energy for a good decision.

Most kids feel sad when their parents separate or divorce. Because it hurts so much to feel sad, some people try to pretend they aren't really sad. One boy's father planned to fly to Mexico for the divorce and to live there afterward. By this choice he had given up custody and cut down on the number of times a year he could see his son. The boy would be in his mother's custody and would have to go for long periods of time without seeing his father. The boy went to a farewell party for his father. Everyone there was acting happy. He knew they expected him to act happy too. He felt miserable. His head ached. Afterward he cried and cried, and he felt better.

By crying over his loss of closeness with his father, he was able to separate himself from his father. After he had cried out the sadness, he thought about his father's leaving. He realized that his father cared more about moving to Mexico than he did about living near him. Now, instead of staying home nursing his headache, he was free to go out and be with his friends, who did want to be with him.

Kids who feel abandoned, as this boy did at first, and kids who feel unprotected, as Carol did when her mother failed to fight for her child support, have to get comfort somewhere.

One girl's parents fought with each other every night over who was to get each of the things in the house. The girl felt lonely, abandoned and forgotten. She found comfort in curling up with her dog to watch TV. Through the weeks of the divorce the routine of taking care of the dog helped her. By caring for an animal, she kept up the routines of her life when so many of the comfortable old patterns were falling apart. She felt warm as she gave her animal warmth.

She enjoyed being able to take care of it. Realizing that the animal's need to be taken care of was even greater than her own, she began to understand that her own helplessness could bring out the same caring in others. She was able to ask her friends for the comfort she needed.

Some kids ease their loneliness and feelings of abandonment by spending time with friends who are going through the same thing. One girl said, "Since my parents started on this divorce I made two new friends. Both of them are going through the same thing. We don't even talk about it much. We just feel better being together."

Sometimes people can be friends and give each other warmth and comfort even if they can't put into words exactly how each one of them feels. Two girls who had helped each other through the loneliness of their parents' divorces met when they were older and talked about their high school years. One remembered the good times they had had together. The other was shocked that her friend didn't recall the loneliness and pain. Even though each didn't really know what the other was feeling during that time, she had still been able to help the other. Each had gotten comfort from knowing that the other was going through the same thing.

Sometimes finding a friend whose parents are also separating can help in another way. Because the friend is going through the same experiences you can talk about it together. You can share your fears, your questions and your hopes.

Two boys' families were at different stages in the divorce process. Each boy was unable to get help in dealing with his problems alone. But together they were able to talk over their problems. Having a friend in the same trouble helped each of them to cope with his own.

The danger of talking over problems with a friend is that you may feel disloyal to your parents. Some parents tell their kids not to talk about family matters outside. Trying to obey this would cut you off from a source of comfort you need right now. If you choose a friend in the same situation, he or she is less likely to gossip or use it against you.

You should tell your parent that you need to talk about it with somebody. If they don't want you to talk about it with a friend or a neighbor, you will need them to help you find a professional person to talk to. Chapter 14 gives you advice on how to find such help.

Another way of coping with the pain during a divorce is to make friends with a warm, happy family. One girl made friends with her piano teacher's family. She stayed after her lessons to share home-baked bread with jam and long talks with her piano teacher's mother and grandmother.

Most often kids find families like that through friends their own age. One boy went home with a friend after school, stayed for dinner and soon found himself going there almost every evening to do his homework and watch TV. He felt more comfortable and relaxed there than he did in his own home. It was a good way to escape the divorce tension in his family.

Another boy enjoyed his girlfriend's house because it was always full of people and talk. She had five brothers and sisters. Holidays at her house were noisy and full of fun. His own family was quiet and solemn. The first Thanksgiving his family didn't spend together, he worried whether to go with his father to his family celebration or with his mother to hers. He solved his problem by spending it at his girlfriend's house. He did what was best for him and he didn't favor either of his parents. He was coping. He was also learning. He learned from his girlfriend's family what his own life could be like in the future.

Girls can find the same kind of comfort with their boyfriends' families. One girl was invited on family outings by her boyfriend's parents. These good times helped to make up for the family life she was missing during the divorce.

Finding friends and other families to be with helps with the sadness and loneliness at the time of a divorce. But not with the anger and resentment. Anger and resentment about the divorce come up even if you don't blame either parent. You are bound to be angry at the situation.

There are ways of working off this anger. One of the best ways is through sports. Active, competitive sports like football, hockey, basketball and soccer give you a chance to use up energy. If you feel like hitting, you can hit a ball. If you feel like kicking, you can kick a ball. You can even grab somebody and throw him on a wrestling mat or a football field. One girl became the handball star of her school as her parents were divorcing. She worked off her anger and resentment on the handball court.

Besides helping to work off anger, sports can help in other ways. At the time of a divorce, everyone in the family suffers some loss of self-confidence. One boy hardly felt like trying in school any more. When his parents gave up on the marriage, he felt like giving up too. He got on the soccer team, and when he became the best player they had, he felt good enough to start trying to write English papers again. Another boy, who felt that everyone in the school knew him as "the kids whose parents are getting divorced," lived that feeling down by becoming a champion skier.

But it isn't necessary to be the best in order to feel better about yourself. Sports can also help you feel better about yourself by giving you a team to be part of. One boy whose parents were separating felt better after he joined his school's baseball team. His family wasn't working together, but his team was.

Team spirit can be felt in other activities besides sports. Putting on a play calls for working together and for cast parties. Being part of a successful production makes you feel like a more successful person. Working on a newspaper or yearbook can give you these same good feelings of belonging. Playing in the school band helped one girl get the attention she needed when her parents were too busy with their own problems to give her very much. Performing made her feel important. After each concert, she shared in the band's applause.

School clubs and student government can give you the extra warmth you may need to help you through the divorce. One girl was elected to student government. She enjoyed staying late after school and working in the student council office. The faculty advisor was motherly without being bossy and there were always kids around to talk to.

Learning any new skill can be helpful at the time of a

separation. Concentrating on that takes your mind off your troubles. While you are learning you feel active. Once you have mastered the skill you feel proud of yourself.

You can use reading, television and movies to get through the hardest times. These can be an escape. When things are really bad, escaping can be the best thing to do. It doesn't solve your problems, but at least it gives you a rest from them. As the characters you see or read about overcome their problems, you may even see ways in which you can overcome yours. Or you may see that theirs are so much worse than yours that yours don't seem so bad.

A diary to write your feelings in can help you over rough spots. Just pouring out how you feel helps. Keeping a continual record helps. Being able to look back at how things were a month ago helps. Other kinds of writing can be useful too. Letters, stories, and poems express feelings. Painting, playing or composing music, dancing and sculpting all express your feelings. You don't need to be talented to release your feelings by creating. You can enjoy the creative act itself.

If you have a special talent you can also take pleasure in seeing other people moved by what you have expressed, and by their applause and approval. One girl acted in a high school production that was so successful the community raised money to send the cast and crew on tour. She got away from the stress at home and found real satisfaction in being part of something that brought enjoyment to other people. For her it was a step on the road to a theatrical career. One boy liked photography. He found a place for himself taking pictures for his college newspaper. This way he was able to attend all kinds of lectures, games, concerts and other events.

He met people he would not otherwise have met. He enjoyed working in the college darkroom to develop his pictures. Working with his hands was a good change from studying. Photography was not his major interest, and he would never be a professional photographer, but it helped him get through a time when he was feeling down.

Some kids cope with their loneliness during the divorce by finding new people to be with. They enlarge their social circle. One boy started playing games again. He bought a pocket chess set so he could start up a game in the student lounge, and even on the school bus. The people he played chess with never became his best friends; he didn't need them to be. But he enjoyed being with them and it eased the loneliness he was feeling at home. His chess-playing later developed into a new source of pleasure for him. He became so good at making friends with new people that he decided to try for a diplomatic career.

Another way to deal with the loneliness and feeling of being short-changed is to get a job. Earning your own money helps you feel independent, and being at the job keeps you out of the house.

One boy got a job as a short-order cook at a local country club. He felt good about earning more money than his friends did. He had fun figuring out the family relationships among the people who ran the business. He liked being with a family that worked together.

Social dancing is another way to enjoy being with people. One girl who felt lonely organized a school dance. The many committee meetings, and the dance itself, kept her around people and gave her a sense of purpose.

Going to school dances, plays, games and concerts can

be a good way of escaping from the stress of being at home. Being there with other people is fun, and it gives you something to talk about afterward.

Even if you aren't doing anything special, it's fun to just be with people you like. Laughing together makes a bond between people. It lets off steam.

Telling jokes helps you talk about what's bothering you without feeling too sorry for yourself. Joking can cut a problem down to a size you can deal with. A joke can make you feel bigger and the problem look smaller. One boy's high school graduation came during his parents' divorce. His mother was there with her boyfriend; his father was there with his girlfriend. Both sets of grandparents were there. The parents of his father's girlfriend were there. So were his mother's boyfriend's parents. He had more parents there than anyone at the graduation. As they trailed him across the school parking lot toward the auditorium doors, he called out to his friends, "Here comes the orphan with his cheering squad!"

Sometimes it helps to have one special friend. A boyfriend or girlfriend can help you feel there is someone in the world who cares about you. It helps to have someone close when you have family trouble. One boy felt better when he was with his girlfriend. His parents' troubles didn't seem so important when he was with someone he really cared about and who really cared about him.

Some kids renew their interest in religion at the time of their parents' separation or divorce. They enjoy church or synagogue social activities, youth group discussions and classes, and the feeling of being part of a kind of family. One girl enjoyed Bible reading with other members of her religious group. She had a good time on weekend retreats to the country with them. She liked the worship, the soul-searching and talking about questions like the meaning of death and evil and the purpose of life.

Just because you prefer to cope one way doesn't mean you can't use other ways too. One girl whose parents had a lot of trouble for a long time used nearly all the ways of coping described in this chapter. She didn't do much crying or yelling, but she got some comfort from cuddling her dog and her hamster. Setting up a place for animals and plants at school and taking care of them also made her feel better. She had many friends. She got close to a few kids who had their own family troubles and one teacher who had grown up in a family like hers. When things got really bad at her house, she moved out for a while and stayed with her best friend's family. She joined the field hockey team. Smashing the ball helped her work off her anger. Winning helped her feel good too. She liked art enough to work on the art staff of the yearbook. She escaped by reading science fiction and fantasy. She kept a journal of her thoughts and feelings and ideas for stories which she sometimes wrote. She didn't play chess or cards, but she did enjoy socializing at school events. She had a good sense of humor and laughed a lot. She didn't have a boyfriend. She got her greatest comfort from the religious group she belonged to. Because she had to learn so many ways of coping during the divorce, she had developed strengths that would always be hers.

Getting through the legal tangle and all the painful feelings about it is only one step toward coping with your

parents' divorce. After that's over, you will have to live the
rest of your life a little differently because you are part of a
separated family.

In the years following the divorce, the pain of separation
has to be expressed and healed so that you and your parents
can get on with your new lives. The agreement your parents
made with their lawyers must be lived up to. But no agreement is perfect. Some parts won't work. These parts must be
changed and new plans made. A divorce will mean the end of
some old ways but also the beginning of many new ones.

# III

*After the Divorce*

# 10

## Living Up to It

The doorbell rang and Chris raced to get it. It was Jane, his father's girlfriend. She looked out of breath as usual.

Lately, ever since he had gotten permission to live with his father, Chris had been trying to talk him into getting married. It would be a family again, just him and Dad and Jane. The other kids could go back to Los Angeles and live with Mom and Mr. Carruthers. He didn't want any of that stepfather business. He was sick of being forced to go on fishing trips just so Mr. Carruthers could prove what a good guy he was.

His father came out of the laundry room with an armful of clothes and a red face.

"Hello," he said. "Look at this, will you?" He held up one of Billy's socks. "Holes! Holes in every pair she sent with them. A new husband making a fat salary and she sends the kids to me for August without enough clothes to get through a week."

"Maybe we can do some shopping," Jane said.

"No, that's their mother's job. But you can see why I get so mad at her."

Chris and his family were trying to live up to his parents' separation agreement. Chris's mother had custody of all four kids. Because their father lived too far away to see them every day or every week, the agreement said that they were to visit him every August. Even though they were living with a stepfather, it was their father's responsibility to support them. He made a small salary himself, but out of it he gave his former wife enough to feed, clothe and house his four sons.

Chris had been in his mother's custody. On this visit he had told his father that he really wanted to be with him. His father didn't know whether to agree to it or not. He felt it might be better for all four boys to be together. He thought about reopening the question to see if a new agreement could be reached. But he knew the boy's mother would never agree to giving up all of them. When he couldn't talk Chris into going back with his brothers, he made up his mind to ask for custody of Chris only.

Chris's mother was upset. She too felt the boys should be together. She felt hurt and rejected because Chris no longer wanted to live with her. First she had lost her husband, now she was about to lose one of her sons.

Chris felt he needed to be with his father. He was still angry with his mother about the divorce. He was still angry with Mr. Carruthers for taking his mother away from his father. He felt they were not people he could be proud of. He wanted to live with his father whom he admired and wanted to be like.

His father couldn't get his mother to agree to the change. So he went back to his lawyer and his lawyer took the case back to court. The judge listened to Chris because he figured he was old enough to know his own mind. He agreed to the custody change.

Sticking to the custody agreement is sometimes hard. It is also hard to judge whether the agreement is being carried out. Judging from the holes in his son's socks, this father decided that his kids were not being given enough clothes. Seeing to it that children have the proper clothes is part of the custody agreement that caused trouble in this family.

In another family, food became the issue. A mother who had custody kept her refrigerator full of soda and snacks but seldom cooked a full meal. The father thought that his kids were not getting good food. He wanted custody.

Custody includes living quarters. A girl lived with her mother in a trailer court. The walk from the school bus stop to her home was dangerous. She felt her living quarters were not good enough. She wanted to live with her father.

One boy needed his teeth straightened. He lived with his mother in a house in the suburbs. He depended on her to drive him to the dentist. When they missed appointments because she was too busy or had forgotten, the boy felt his mother was letting him down by not getting him proper medical care.

Giving proper guidance is the hardest part of custody. It includes seeing that young children are not left alone, that all children go to school, that they are protected from harmful influences and taught the difference between right and wrong. One girl stayed home from school to care for her sick younger brother. The girl understood her mother's problem. If she stayed home from work too often she would lose her job. Her mother had to choose between leaving the younger child alone and keeping her daughter out of school. Whatever she did would be against the rules of custody.

Custody means protecting kids from harmful influences. A boy whose father had custody got in with a group of kids who were using drugs. His father felt that he had to forbid the boy to see these kids to protect him from their bad influence. He felt this was the only way he could stick to his custody agreement. The boy felt this was unfair. His friends' parents didn't stop them. Why should his parent have to be more strict than the others?

One girl in Chicago had been in joint custody of both her parents. Her mother decided to move to Mexico. She wanted to go with her mother. Her father tried to sue to prevent them from moving because it would make the joint custody impossible. He couldn't help make the decisions from so far away. The judge decided to give custody to the girl's mother since joint custody really couldn't work any more. The girl and her mother moved to Mexico.

Another boy had been living with his mother, his grandmother and his aunt. He felt they were spoiling him and making him soft and weak. He began to feel lonesome with no man around. He wanted to be with his father to become tougher. He also felt his lonely father needed him.

A girl wanted to be with her father because she felt her brother was her mother's favorite. With her father she would be the special one. She had to give up that idea because her father really couldn't take care of her. He was a musician who played dance jobs and concerts in many cities. He was always on the move. The girl stayed with her mother and brother. She learned to cope with her mother's favoritism. She had to.

Custody agreements are always special. In general, it is a good idea for kids in a family to stay together, but for Chris, it was not a good idea. He had a special need to be with his father. His anger at his mother and his stepfather would have made it hard for him to stay with them. He didn't find this out until after he had tried the first custody arrangement. So the original agreement had to be changed.

The girl whose mother moved needed a new custody arrangement because her life had changed. Many custody changes are the result of changes in the family situation. Remarriage, new jobs, and moving are often reasons for change of custody.

The boy whose father was alone needed a change of custody because he himself was changing as he grew up. As he got closer to manhood, he wanted to be more like his father and he thought his father would understand his needs better.

The girl who wanted to be with her musician father couldn't get custody changed. Her mother refused and her father wouldn't ask for custody because he knew he couldn't handle it. The judge, knowing that the father couldn't give her a stable home life, would not have awarded it anyway.

Parents have to live up to the visiting plan as well as the custody arrangement in their separation agreement. Chris's family had agreed on a month-long visit every August. At the end of one summer visit, the kids asked if they could stay for an extra week. Their father was delighted. He had to call their mother for permission because the length of their visit was part of the divorce agreement. Everyone was very disappointed when she said no. Their father was angry. The parents quarreled over the phone. To the kids it sounded just like the bad old times of marriage battles before the divorce.

Their mother was upset because she and her new husband and the kids were supposed to go on a vacation of their own that week. She had already made the reservations for all of them. It was the only time her husband had off from work. Their father was upset because he hated to let them go. He knew he wouldn't see them again for another whole year.

The visitation plan is the hardest part to live up to in the separation agreement. It requires new decisions all the time. Because they are not going to see each other again for a while, parents and kids feel they must make the most of every moment. Under the pressure of knowing that their time together is limited, they feel they have to plan each visit beforehand: to decide where to go and what to do. This puts a strain on the relationship. At the end of the visit, if it's been good, kids and the parent they are visiting often feel like staying together. The better the visit has been, the harder it is to leave.

One boy had to choose between going to a basketball game with his friends and being with his father. He could have gone to the game with his father, but it wouldn't have been the same. He would have felt strange that his friends saw him there with his father. He decided to go to the game with his friends and not see his father. But during the game he felt guilty. It spoiled some of his good time. He knew that he and his friends could get together any time, but his father could only see him on the one visiting day.

Another boy had trouble sticking to his parents' agreement about holidays. The agreement said that if he spent Thanksgiving with one parent, he would spend Christmas with the other. On the first Christmas eve after his parents' divorce he was scheduled to go to a party with his father. But he felt like staying home with his mother, who was alone.

Deciding whether to go was very hard for him. He went to the party with his father, but during the party he felt guilty about leaving his mother. His parents' agreement seemed fair when they made it. But it didn't feel fair that night. Whatever he did, he would be hurting one of his parents. Yet it wasn't his fault. He hadn't divorced anybody.

Some visits turn into chores. Sometimes it's hard to find anything to talk about. The visiting parent may have been hard to talk to anyway; now that they don't share daily life there is less to talk about. On visits they need to do something together to give them something to talk about.

One girl who was in her father's custody had a long visit with her mother on a cross-country bus tour. The mother had planned and saved for this trip all year. They had lots of new experiences but they didn't really share them. They never talked over what they had seen and done. The girl felt no closer to her mother at the end than she had at the beginning. Because the visit was such a special production they were too tense to enjoy it. They were both bound to be disappointed.

One boy had his best visit with his father when he showed his father around the grounds of the summer camp he worked at. They had something real to talk about. They shared an experience.

*After the Divorce*

Parting after a good visit can hurt. Chris and his brothers found that out when they couldn't stay the extra week with their father. When that happens, the agreement may need to be changed. Longer visits or joint custody may help.

The child support part of the agreement is sometimes harder for parents to live up to than they thought it would be. One boy's parents agreed to put a certain amount of money into a bank account for their son's college education. The boy thought his college education was all paid for. But when tuition costs went up, he had no money to finish. He felt let down by his parents because they didn't plan ahead for rising costs. His parents made a new agreement; but he couldn't trust them as much anymore. He realized they weren't as wise as he thought they were.

A girl's father lost his job. He was lucky to get a new one even at a lower salary. He had to ask for reduced support. The girl felt angry at losing most of her clothes allowance. She hated not having money for good times with her friends. She felt sorry for her father too.

One girl found it hard to live with her parents' agreement. Since her mother got little child support, they had to move to a small apartment. She resented not having her own room, not having enough closet space and losing her old friends. She felt sorry for her mother and knew her father was giving all he could, but she was furious at the situation she found herself in.

Even if the amount of support in the agreement was large enough, changes in the cost of living may make it too small. The parent getting the support may not be able to buy enough food and clothing when costs go up. Unexpected medical and dental bills may add to the cost of support. A

parent on a tight budget may not have enough money to
increase the support to cover such bills. Your parents may
know ways to make what money they have go further.
Medical and dental care may be covered by insurance.
Clinics give low cost or free care if you can't afford to pay for
it.

Sometimes you can earn what you need. If your child
support isn't quite enough, you may be able to make the
difference between what you get and what you need. One boy
typed other kids' term papers. A girl started a catering service, hiring out to help at parties. Another girl did sketches of
people on a commission basis.

Living up to the custody, visiting, and child support
parts of the agreement can become complicated.

A seventeen-year-old boy wanted his own car. His
mother was delighted that they couldn't afford one because
she was afraid he would drive too fast. On a visit to his father
he mentioned that his friend wanted to sell an old car for
$200. His father slipped him the money as he left. He bought
the car. His mother was upset. Who would pay the insurance? She accused his father of misusing his visiting rights.
She said he was interfering with her custody. She complained
that he should have given that money for child support or put
it in the bank for his son's education. The boy felt guilty; he
felt he had gone behind his mother's back. The father felt
bad. He had just wanted to do something nice for his son.

They could have talked it over. The mother might have
agreed to let him have a car after he took driver's education.
The father could have agreed to wait to give him the money
until then. The boy could have agreed to work to pay the
insurance.

Getting the parents together to talk it over would have been the hardest part. But talking it over beforehand could prevent trouble later. Sticking to the agreement takes a lot of talking over decisions before they are made. All the people affected by the agreement have to have their say to make sure that the decision is a fair one. The mother had custody, but the boy wanted his father to be part of the decision. If this happened often, he might ask for joint custody.

After a divorce, parents and kids have the separation agreement or divorce decree to guide them in their changed relationships to each other. Rules about custody, child support and visitation help them to adjust to their new lives. But there are no rules to guide kids in their changed relationships to brothers and sisters and other relatives, old and new, after a divorce. There are no rules for feelings.

# 11

## The Family Circle

Sally hoisted herself over the pool edge to flop down on her towel. She liked it here at her father's new house. She loved using the pool. The food was good. They had a room for her with an extra bed so she could bring a friend. Everything here was so much better than the apartment she and her mother shared. Even her stepmother, Phyllis, was prettier and better dressed than her mother. Yet she hated herself for comparing.

"C'mon, Sally, I'll race you to the end of the pool."

She looked up. Her stepbrother, Tony, was grinning down at her. "Okay. Loser vacuums the pool today."

She took a racing dive and splashed in. By the time she got to the other end, Tony was climbing up the ladder and shaking the water out of his hair. "Too bad, Sally," he said. "Want a hand up?"

The screen door opened and she heard her father's voice, then Phyllis's. She looked up.

"What's the good word, son?" her father said.

Sally winced. It was just a word. Tony wasn't his son, but it hurt every time she heard her father say it.

"I got my Harvard application almost done."

"Need any help with it?"

"No thanks. I just have to polish up the essay and type it."

"Hear that, Sally? Tony's going to be a Harvard man."

"Yes." Sally sat up and put on her sunglasses. "I hope you get in, Tony."

"Get in?" her father said. "Don't worry. He'll get in."

"How about you, honey? Phyllis said you had something to tell me."

"It can wait, Dad. Till after dinner anyway." Forever, she was thinking. It could wait forever. How could she tell him she was flunking math when Tony was going to Harvard?

When Sally's father remarried, he got not only a wife but also a son. He and his new wife, putting their resources together, also had a lot more money than Sally and her mother. His new wife already had a house. When Sally's parents divorced, they had to sell their house, and Sally and her mother took a small apartment so they could afford to live on the child support and maintenance they would get.

Sally envied her stepbrother. He hadn't had to give up the house he had grown up in. She envied her father's new wife. It seemed as if Phyllis had everything. She resented her mother for not having been able to get that kind of life for herself and Sally. She resented her father for not having given them enough money so they could have kept their own house. Besides all that, Sally was jealous of her stepbrother's and stepmother's closeness with her father. When her father asked about Tony's Harvard application, Sally was jealous. When her father kissed his new wife, Sally had to look away. She wished she could just enjoy her visits with her father and not spoil them with so much envy.

When parents remarry, kids are bound to feel jealous of the new husband or wife and envious of whatever they have. Some kids feel they want to share in the new life their parents have begun. Other kids just don't want any part of it.

One girl enjoyed going to visit her father in the apartment he shared with his girlfriend and her daughter. She hated going back home to her mother and brother. She would have liked to stay and be part of the new family. But she couldn't. Her father and his girlfriend were not married, and her mother wouldn't give her father a divorce. In the separation agreement her mother had been given custody. No court would have allowed this girl to live with her father.

A boy whose father was thinking of remarrying refused to meet his father's girlfriend and her two sons. He said, "When he marries her, I'll meet her. Right now, he's not married to her. She's nothing to me." The boy felt that having one mother was enough. If he had to have a step-mother also, he thought he could accept that. But he didn't want to have to meet a string of possible stepmothers. And he didn't want to be saddled with the responsibility of having to approve his father's choice of a new wife. He felt it would be disloyal to his mother if he were to help choose her replacement.

Another boy wouldn't go near the house where his mother lived with her new husband and his children. He couldn't stand to see his mother with anyone but his father. He wound up living with his father and seeing his mother only when they could meet outside her home.

Many kids feel uncomfortable when their parents start dating or remarry—especially if they choose younger partners. One girl felt uncomfortable bringing her friends home when her stepmother was there. Her stepmother was too young. She didn't look like a mother. A boy whose father remarried a much younger woman was uneasy when his stepmother tried to give him advice. She didn't know enough. He felt he ought to be giving *her* advice.

Parents and stepparents are the basis of the family, but many kids actually spend more time with their brothers and sisters than with their parents. Relationships between brothers and sisters change after a divorce or separation. The most obvious kind of change is the shift in responsibilities.

One of the kids may take over some family responsibilities of the parent who is no longer there. The chores that used to be done by the now-absent parent may be given to one of the kids or may be divided up among all of them.

Many kids grow closer to their brothers and sisters after a separation. They give each other the warmth and support they used to get from the parent who is no longer there. They also try to make up for the loss of warmth and support from the parent they live with while that parent is adjusting to a new life. Other kids pull away from their brothers and sisters at this time.

In one family the kids were left alone more after the divorce. With their father living far away and their mother working longer hours, they had no one to help them with their homework, no one to tell what had happened that day in school—except each other. The two sisters counted on each other more than they ever had before. They gave each other the attention they used to get from their mother.

In another family the father had always been the one blamed for everything that went wrong. If a car passed him on the highway, everyone agreed he was driving too slow. If he passed another car, he was driving too fast. After he left the home, the family had to look for somebody else to blame. The brother who had been closest to the father began to be blamed for everything. He tried desperately to defend himself, putting the blame on the oldest brother. After the divorce, each of these boys spent lots of time and energy trying to avoid being labeled the "bad one" in the family. Their former closeness turned sour.

One girl in a family with two younger brothers decided to live with her father after her parents' separation. Her father had married her favorite teacher from school. She felt close to her father and her new stepmother. They were interested in the same things that she liked. She found it more and more difficult to keep on visiting her mother and her two brothers, especially as her own social life took up more and more of her time. Later, she was able to get closer to her mother again. But she was never able to make up for not having been part of her brothers' growing-up years.

When parents remarry, the stepparent may have children. Having new kids in the family changes everybody's place. Each of the families used to have an oldest child. Now only one can be the oldest. Each used to have a youngest. Now only one can have this place.

One boy's mother married a man who had a son just the same age as the boy's older brother. The boy had always gotten along with his own older brother. But now he had two of them. When they were all together, he felt they were ganging up on him. He wished there were someone his own age for him to team up with.

A girl had always been the leader in her family because she was the oldest. When both her parents remarried, she wasn't the oldest in either family. Her mother's husband had a son who was older than she; he became her older brother. And her father's wife had an older daughter. Now she wasn't even the oldest girl. She felt as if she had lost her special place in the family. She went off to boarding school because she no longer felt at home in either family.

One girl really got mad at her new younger brother when he started messing up things in her room. Her older brother and sister used to complain about her getting into their things. Now she was outraged because her new little brother had used her special drawing pencils to write on the walls.

When the remarriage produces a baby, there may be other feelings. Many kids feel jealous when their parents have babies. They think their parents are too old for sex. They resent the baby because it is proof of their parents' sex life.

One girl worried when her father's wife became pregnant. She had been jealous of her new stepmother. She was afraid that her father would care less about her when the baby came. Would her father and stepmother stop paying attention to her? Would they have to give up their weekend hikes when the baby came? Would the new baby take too much time?

She was shocked at her own reaction. Her feelings couldn't have anything to do with the baby itself. There was no baby yet. What bothered her most was her fear that she would lose the mothering of her stepmother. She had never thought her father's wife mattered. She had always called her by her first name; she never thought of her as her mother. She had a mother of her own. But now she was feeling as jealous as her friends felt when their mothers had babies.

How important stepmothers and stepfathers are in kids' lives depends on how young the kids are when their parents remarry. If your parent were to remarry when you were already an adult, you would probably think of the person as "my mother's husband" or "my father's wife." If your parent were to remarry while you were a young child, you would have much stronger feelings about your stepparent. If your parent were to remarry while you were in your teens, the relationship could go either way. One boy really welcomed his new stepfather. He felt at home with him because he had known him almost all his life. His stepfather helped him through a rough time when his own father was too hurt to even keep in touch with him.

Another boy couldn't stand his stepfather, who had all kinds of rules for what people could and couldn't do. He punished the boy for breaking the rules, even when the boy didn't know what they were. The longer the boy lived with his mother and her new husband, the worse it seemed to get. He said, "My stepfather used to be mean only when he was sick. Now he's mean all the time."

Kids have always felt suspicious and resentful of stepparents. Think of all the ''wicked stepmothers'' in fairy
tales. Most kids are afraid that stepparents will favor their
own children. This idea is partly realistic. Many people do
think their own children are better than anyone else's.

But some kids find that they get along better with their
stepparents than with their own parents. One boy said, ''I
really like my stepfather. When my mother told me she was
getting married, I was glad to have someone in the house
again.'' That boy had not heard from his own father for a long
time.

Some stepparents get along with their stepchildren better than with their own children. A boy said of his stepfather,
''I can't figure out why his own kids don't want to live with
him instead of with their mother.''

Other kids have real trouble getting along with their
stepparents because they can't see them for what they are.
They take their feelings about their own parents and transfer
them to their stepparents. They see their stepparents as having all the bad traits they can't stand to see in their own
parents. A girl whose own mother criticized her all the time
felt that her stepmother was too critical. A boy who wanted
more of his mother's time and attention complained that his
stepmother was always pushing him out of the house.

Like new brothers and sisters, stepparents are often
relatives you live with. Because you will be with them every
day or visit with them every weekend, they become very
important in your life. This is why parents who wish to
remarry often ask you for your opinion of the person they are
considering. They may want to make sure that you can be
comfortable with their new partner before they make a final

decision. If you have an opinion and are asked for it, you owe it to yourself and to your parent to be honest. You can't tell your parent what to do, but voicing your hopes beforehand can help that parent make a decision you can all live with.

Once a parent has remarried, you have to adjust to your new stepparent. If you can't form a close relationship, at least you can work out a bearable arrangement.

One girl's father remarried a woman the girl didn't particularly like. The girl remained in her father's custody but worked out an arrangement that allowed her to spend most of her time either at boarding school or summer camp. Her older sister worked out a different arrangement. She asked for a custody change so that she could live with her mother. The two boys in the family were satisfied to stay with their father and new stepmother.

Divorce permanently changes the family circle. One parent moves away. Remarriage brings new parents and often new brothers and sisters into the circle. Relationships which had been worked out in the original family now must be worked out again. Whatever a lost family member contributed must be given by others. New family members must make places for themselves. This is always hard to do.

When your own immediate family is changing, you may find yourself getting closer to other relatives. They may be able to give you more attention. They may have the time to be with you when you might otherwise be lonely. If you feel that your family life has been shattered, your grandparents' memories can help you see the continuity of your life. Asking older relatives for their memories of your parents when they were young can be a way to get to know your own roots better at a time when you feel you have been uprooted.

One girl enjoyed vacations with her grandmother after her parents' divorce. Her grandmother took her to resorts her mother couldn't afford. She felt special because her grandmother wanted her company. She got special clothes and was fussed over. She knew that her grandmother was pleased to have the company of someone young and lively.

A boy loved going fishing with his uncle. His parents were divorced when he was very young. He felt that he hardly knew his father, who moved far away after the divorce. His uncle's stories about how he and the boy's father used to go fishing together helped the boy feel closer to his father.

If one or both of your parents remarry, you may have new grandparents. New grandparents can add to your life even though they may bring a whole new set of problems.

A boy whose own grandparents loved to baby him enjoyed being with his stepmother's mother. She was a dean at a local college. When he visited her on campus, she would take him to lunch at the faculty club. She had never known him as a little kid, so she treated him as she would any of the college students. It was a good change.

Another boy was not so lucky. He overheard his grandmother-to-be tell her husband that she felt her son had taken on too much responsibility in marrying a woman with five children. It made him feel uncomfortable and unwanted. These grandparents did not live with the family, so the boy was able to avoid them.

A girl got closer to an aunt after her parents' divorce. She went over to her aunt's house after school to avoid the silence in her own house now that her mother worked full-time.

A boy whose father moved into an apartment house owned by his family found that he grew closer to many of his relatives. His father's three brothers lived in the building with their wives and children. The boy was surrounded by uncles, aunts and cousins. He liked the constant visiting back and forth and always having someone to talk to.

But not all families draw closer after a divorce. One girl resented the fact that her father's large close-knit family left her out of their holiday celebrations. After her parents' divorce she was living with her mother, who had no family at all. She and her mother joined friends for Thanksgiving and other holidays.

A boy who was away at school wrote to his mother: "I've written to everyone in the family, but the only ones who answer are you and Dad." His family just avoided the uncomfortable feelings about the divorce by avoiding him. He asked his mother to urge his relatives to write, even if they didn't have anything special to say. They enjoyed the letters he wrote them in return.

Another boy, who lived with his mother, found that his father's mother wrote to him less and saw him much less than before. She sent fewer presents at birthdays and holidays. His father's brother and sister and their children never called or wrote to him. He felt cut off from half his family.

If part of your family acts like this, it may be because they are not sure of their place in your life. They may think that because you have chosen to live with one parent, you don't want to be part of the other parent's family. If you call or write them, they may be happy to hear from you. If they aren't, you will be no more cut off from them than you were before.

The larger family is especially important at holidays, birthdays and special times like weddings, funerals and graduations. Those are the times for big family parties. Keeping up the family ties after a divorce can keep you from losing the warmth and sense of belonging that a large family can give. In smaller families each member is even more important than in very large families, so keeping up the ties is also more important.

After a divorce your family circle changes. There may be more people or fewer. They may be different people. Your relationships with the people who have been in your family all along change too. It takes time and energy to settle down into your changed family circle.

# 12

---

# Settling Down

---

Linda bent over to tie her shoe. Really, she just wanted to hide her face. She thought she was going to cry. She didn't want anyone to see how upset she was, especially since her sister Donna was standing there with her mother and Carlos looking as if the whole thing didn't bother her at all. As if she didn't care that the luggage was already on the plane and their mother was going off on a trip with her boyfriend. Donna was smiling and wishing them a good time.

How *could* she? Linda thought. Didn't she care that Dad was alone in his apartment? Didn't she care that she and Linda were going to be alone for two weeks or maybe longer? Her mother's "maybe longer" had really stung. Suppose she and Carlos decided to stay in Puerto Rico and settle there? Suppose they never came back?

After Linda's parents divorced, her mother seemed to change. She seemed younger. She began dating men much younger than Linda's father. She wasn't home as much. Linda was alone more and more. This was the first time her mother had gone away since the divorce, but seeing her mother board the plane with Carlos brought together everything Linda had been feeling since her father moved out. She felt alone and abandoned. Her father was gone, and the mother she had always known had changed into somebody new.

Linda knew that her mother would come back, but part of her still thought, "What if she doesn't? What if this new person chooses a completely new life?" Linda got some comfort from calling her father and being with her sister. She also got comfort from all the things in her life that hadn't changed. These were things outside the family, like her school, her friends and her church youth group. But she was afraid that if people learned about her mother's trip with her boyfriend they might disapprove. They might turn away from both her mother and her. If that happened she thought her life would be ruined. She was afraid the changes in her mother would lead to disaster in her own life.

Parents are likely to change after a divorce. Many parents, especially if they don't remarry right away, are likely to change their looks and their interests and hobbies. While they were married, both partners adjusted their dress, their hairstyles, their food, furniture and even their friends to each other's taste. When they become single again, they are free to express their own tastes.

A mother who didn't work while she was married is

likely to get a job. A father who didn't pay much attention to his appearance before may lose weight, get new clothes, grow a new mustache or shave off an old one. They may enroll in adult education courses or go back to school for diplomas or degrees.

Some parents make changes mostly in their social life. With their new-found freedom, they might suddenly start dating many different people; or they might look for one person to take the place of the one they have divorced.

The changes parents make in their own lives affect the other members of the family. Sometimes kids don't like the changes in their parents. Suddenly they seem too young, too interested in themselves, too busy with their own activities. At other times kids really enjoy sharing their parents' new lives.

One girl's mother rented a typewriter so that she could brush up her typing skills before going out to look for a job. The girl took advantage of this by teaching herself to type. She felt closer to her mother than she had when her parents were living together. Her mother was now someone she could want to be like. Her own growing up was moved ahead by her mother's new interest.

A fifteen-year-old boy got a chance to go to Europe when his mother started traveling after the divorce. His father had never liked traveling. The boy got an extra advantage from his mother's new independence.

Another boy hated the changes in his father's appearance after the divorce. His father used to wear the same old clothes till they wore out. Now he had a whole new wardrobe of young-looking outfits. The boy thought he looked silly.

His father used to be someone he could ask for advice, someone he could rely on to have his best interests in mind. But now his father seemed more like a competitor. His young clothes made him look like he was interested in young girls. The boy was no longer comfortable around him. His father now seemed like someone who might be competing with him for the same girls.

A sixteen-year-old girl whose mother went back to school resented having to fix dinner for herself and the younger kids while her mother was at evening classes. The girl felt used. She felt as if now she was being the mother and her mother was acting like a daughter. She was glad her mother was back in school, but she didn't like being forced into growing up faster than she felt ready for.

In a larger family all the kids took turns fixing dinner so their mother would be able to commute to a new job in the city. Before the divorce their father had shared in the cooking. Afterward the kids enjoyed taking over. One of the boys even became a gourmet cook. He was making up for the loss of his father by carrying on with something that his father had done.

In all these cases family relationships changed after the divorce. The place of each parent in the family changed and so did the place of each of the kids.

Parents change their relationships to the larger world outside the family after a divorce. They may leave some groups they used to belong to and join others. They may become more active in groups they have always belonged to. They may begin dating.

One boy's mother joined a new church after her divorce.

The one she had belonged to before didn't approve of divorce. After her divorce she felt like an outcast there, so she left that church. Later, she found another religious group that welcomed her. When she remarried, members of the congregation brought food and flowers for her wedding reception. By coming and celebrating, they made the marriage seem okay. The boy enjoyed the wedding. He felt like part of a large, warm family.

Another boy's mother went back to school after the divorce. She made new friends in her classes and began to see them socially. She was away from home more often, but when she was home, the house was often filled with interesting people. The boy enjoyed meeting them and talking to them.

One girl who was an only child had a father who got very interested in his work after his divorce. He wasn't home very much. He didn't have time to visit with her. When they did have time together he didn't want to go anyplace or do anything because he was exhausted all the time. She got mad and stopped visiting him.

One boy had a mother who had always wanted to work for political causes. Before the divorce her husband kept her from speaking in public about politics. He didn't want his name linked with her causes. After the divorce, she became very active. She even ran for office. At first the boy felt left out. Then he got involved too. He began to be proud of his mother.

Another boy's father finally had time to join the tennis club. He was free on weekends now that he didn't have to do yardwork or home repairs. The boy had always loved tennis and was a good player. He was glad to see his father moving to this new interest.

Some of their parents' new interests are not so easy for kids to accept. The most difficult change for most kids is when their parents begin dating.

One boy's mother asked him directly, "What would you think if I started going out with a man?"

The boy thought a minute and then said, "I don't care. As long as he's an okay guy. As long as he's not somebody awful." He really didn't want the responsibility of deciding what his mother should do with her life. He felt she was being childish. She was an adult. She should have been able to decide such things for herself. Why was she dragging him into it? He was adult enough not to ask her advice about his girlfriends.

Another girl felt awkward when her mother's dates came to the house to pick her up. She and her two sisters watched over the stairs to see the men her mother went out with, but they refused to come down and meet any of them. The girls enjoyed making fun of their mother's boyfriends.

One girl's father wanted her to babysit for the children of the woman he was dating. This made her very angry. They weren't even her own brother and sister. She didn't see why she should give up her Saturday nights to be with them.

One fourteen-year-old boy refused to go to the movies with his mother and her boyfriend and his two children. The children were much younger than he. He would have felt out of place. He wanted to go to the movies with his own girlfriend.

All of these kids felt uncomfortable about their parents'

dating. Any kid is bound to feel jealous and abandoned when a parent begins to date.

Kids feel especially protective if their mother begins dating. Because the mother is the one who usually takes care of the infant, both girls and boys find it harder throughout life to separate from their mothers. When a mother dates, her kids lose some of her interest, time, and attention. Seeing her go out with a man recalls the painful feeling of having to share her with someone. It is like the feeling the infant experiences in sharing her with the father.

In addition to the feelings that *all* kids have about their mothers' dates, girls are especially jealous of their fathers' dates and boys of their mothers' dates. A girl who sees her father go out on dates feels as if she is losing a man she loves to another woman. A boy feels the same way when his mother begins to date.

These feelings of anger and resentment don't have to continue. When you recognize such feeling in yourself, you can make them less painful in two ways. First, you can get more involved socially with your own friends. Kids who have plenty going on in their own lives feel less envious of their parents' good times and less jealous of the people their parents date. Second, you can make friends with the people your parents date. When a parent settles down to a steady relationship with one person, you can share experiences that can be recalled later and make you feel like part of each other's lives.

Some kids' parents have their dates stay with them overnight. One boy's mother had many different people over. The boy hated them all. He hated her door being closed in the morning. He hated having to tiptoe around in his own house. He especially hated it when his mother would have an argument with one of her boyfriends because he couldn't help hearing their raised voices. He had tried making friends with the first two or three of them, but it was so awful when they broke up with his mother and he didn't see them anymore that he didn't even want to say hello to any of the new ones. Another girl with the same problem solved it by asking to have custody changed.

Sometimes a parent's date turns into a steady relationship. Kids who have been used to having a parent all to themselves after a divorce may resent having to share this parent with another person. And the new person may resent the kids. Sometimes the new person may make demands on kids that they can't or won't meet.

One boy got angry at his mother's boyfriend, who kept wanting to teach him how to fly a plane. He wanted to spend the time with his own friends. He suspected that the man wanted him to be the son he had never had. The boy had a father of his own and he resented anyone trying to take his father's place.

One girl was surprised when her father's steady girlfriend bought her a cashmere sweater. She loved the sweater, but it wasn't her birthday or a special occasion. She hadn't done anything to deserve a gift. She felt used. She thought her father's friend was really trying to win her over so that she would speak well of her to her father. She didn't like anyone trying to bribe her that way.

Two sisters who played piano and guitar hated being forced to keep quiet because their mother's steady boyfriend wanted to read his newspaper in their living room. They were angry because he didn't even live there. What right did he have to tell them how to live?

Parents often develop steady relationships with new partners as they settle down after a divorce. Kids have to learn to live with this fact of their parents' new lives.

Some kids' parents have their new partners move in with them. People who have been divorced are especially likely to want to be sure they can share their life and a home with their new partner before they marry again. They may do this as a trial marriage to see how it would be living together if they did get married. At least they can tell if it would be impossible. Some kids feel ashamed if their parents are living with someone without being married. They feel awkward about introducing the person their parent is living with to their friends. They don't know what to call the person. Do they say, "This is Richard, my mother's boyfriend"? That would be misleading because he's more than a boyfriend. He lives there. "My mother's lover" would be embarrassing because many people think having a lover is immoral. "My mother's roommate" would make people laugh. "My mother's friend" is true but doesn't tell the whole story. "This is Richard. He lives here" is the easiest to say, but may lead to further questions, like "Who's Richard to you? Why does he live with you?"

The best answer is the truth. You can say, "He lives with my mother." If your friends want to stay away from you after that, you have some choices. You can try explaining to your friends that it is your mother's choice, not yours. Or you can ask for a change of custody. Or you can stay where you are and try to make new friends.

Whether you are going to be embarrassed by your

parents' choices depends a lot on where you live. If all your neighbors think divorce is sinful, if none of your friends have had a parent who lived with a lover, if the people in your town think it's wrong for divorced parents to date and your parent actually does these things, you are going to be ashamed or embarrassed. You may feel like an outcast. But if some of your neighbors have made the same choices, you are less likely to be embarrassed.

There are some situations that will be uncomfortable in almost any community. One is where the parent chooses a partner of the same sex. Outside of certain sections of large cities, this is likely to be thought peculiar.

Kids whose parents set up housekeeping with lovers of the same sex have the same problems as kids whose parents are living with people they are not married to. They also have special problems. One special problem is their fear that they may become homosexual themselves. But kids don't become homosexual because their parents are.

The scariest part of having a person living with your parent while you are still at home is the fear that you may be seduced. Some kids are teased or forced into having sex with older people. A person who is around the house when you may be undressed or only partly dressed is a special threat.

One girl was afraid to stay home on the night her mother went out to her pottery class. She was afraid to be alone with her mother's lover. He was too close to her own age and too attractive. She liked him so much that she was afraid she could be persuaded to have sex with him. If that happened she knew she would feel awful. She would feel disloyal to her mother and would be unable to go on living at home.

If the parent you are living with has a new partner living in the house, you may have to be especially careful. You must be able to prevent yourself from being drawn into more than you are ready for.

Some of the things you can do are: avoid being alone together, try not to flirt, keep your clothes on whenever you're outside your own room. If you feel uneasy, talk about it with your own parent. If anything you don't like happens, complain. If complaining doesn't work, yell. If that doesn't work, tell the parent you are not living with. If you can't do any of these things, get outside help immediately. Your local hospital emergency room may have a counselor or social worker you can talk to. That person can help you decide what to do. If you are forced into any kind of sexual act, you may need medical treatment. The last chapter will tell you more about getting such help.

As parents move out into the world, kids sometimes feel lonely. Some kids feel pushed out of their parents' lives.

One boy's father took a job in another town after his divorce. The boy's brother was married and already out of the house. His father sent the boy to a boarding school. He felt pushed out.

Feeling pushed aside is a problem. Settling down into your own life is the solution. Moving into a world apart from your parents is the way to settle into your own life. All kids need to get separate from their families. Most kids from divorced families separate more easily than other kids because the divorce forces them to see their parents as people rather than just as parents. But some kids from divorced families find it even harder to separate. Kids get separate from their parents by beginning to see them not as gods but as real people with flaws. When parents are not around it's easier to idealize them. Real parents with real flaws are easier to leave than idealized images of absent parents.

One girl was sent to boarding school when her father remarried. She quickly settled down and made friends. She loved the school. She felt she'd never be lonely again with so many kids around all the time. For this girl, separation was made easier by her parents' divorce.

Many kids join youth groups, after-school clubs and other programs to help them get through the divorce period. But after the divorce most kids find that staying in these groups for a short time is not enough. They need to settle down. They need to choose the things they most like to do, the groups they most like being part of, and to stay with those until they get the comfortable, old-shoe feeling of belonging.

One girl worked on costumes for a school play. She liked it so much that she decided to cut down on some of her other activities so that she could give more time to the drama group and work on costumes for all the school productions. She liked the people and the surroundings. She liked being known as the costume designer. She knew she was needed and that they would call on her again. This feeling was more important to her than being in five or six different activities and not being known strongly for any one of them. The ongoing relationships in the drama group helped her cope with the changes in her family.

One boy decided to stay in high school for his senior

year even though he could have managed to graduate early. Coping with the changes in his family was hard enough. He didn't feel ready to move on yet. He needed another year with his old friends. His friends gave him a connection to his own past.

Many kids feel ashamed after their parents' divorce. They feel different. They may not know any other kids with divorced parents. They don't realize how many of them there are.

One boy felt ashamed of his parents' divorce until he moved to the city with his mother. In his new school, over half the kids had parents who were either separated or divorced.

Some of the shame that kids feel comes from the way other people behave toward them. Many people feel divorce is wrong. They feel that people who divorce are selfish or even sinful. These people feel that no matter how bad a marriage is, a couple should stay together. People who feel like this may stay away from divorced parents and their children.

Some people think divorce is a tragedy. They expect both kids and parents from divorced families to be miserable. They don't want to be around misery. So they stay away. They don't realize that people are often happier after a divorce than before.

People who are having marriage trouble themselves are sometimes afraid to be around divorced people. They are afraid the idea of divorce will become too attractive if they see people who have survived it.

Still other people think that divorce means failure and that people who divorce are losers. They don't want to be associated with failures, so they stay away. Kids can be hurt by people who stay away from them after their parents' divorce if they believe that these people are right.

You may feel that people are staying away from you after your parents' divorce and not know why. If you think that it might be for one of these reasons, you could ask your friends, if they are close enough. You could ask them what's the matter and why aren't they dropping in or calling you any more.

You might get a straight answer. A friend might even say, "My parents told me I can't see you any more because your parents are divorced." If this should happen, you will know that the friendship wasn't lost because of anything you said or did. It's their problem, not yours. You can move on and make new friends.

You might not get a straight answer. Your friend might be too embarrassed to tell you the reason. If there is no other reason, you can figure it's probably because of the divorce. If your friend isn't even willing to tell you, then there's not that much friendship there. You'd be better off with a new friend.

Lots of kids find that it's easier to make friends after a divorce with other kids who have gone through the same thing. Most kids settle down better after a divorce if they know at least one other kid from a divorced family to talk to and compare themselves with.

One boy whose father was away for five years and then came back said, "I have a friend whose father has been gone for nine years and he never even heard from him."

Some kids are so ashamed of their parents' divorce that they try to hide it. They may even hide it from people who could help them cope with it better if only they knew what was going on.

One girl began cutting school after her parents' divorce. She had just moved to a new neighborhood. Some kids at her new school asked her to cut school with them and go to the movies. She went. If her father had been living at home, she would never have done such a thing. She was too afraid of her father's disapproval. But now she was mad at both her father and her mother. She wanted to get even with them. Later, when her guidance counselor asked her, "Is anything wrong at home?" She said, "No. Nothing. Everything's just the same as usual." The whole story came out only when her mother went to school to find out why her grades were so low.

A boy spent all his time in school nodding or napping. He had taken an evening job in a gas station to help support his mother and sister after his father left them. He was so ashamed that his father had abandoned the family that he never told anyone at school he was working. He was very much criticized for falling asleep at school, and his grades suffered. If he had told his school guidance counselor, he might have been able to get work experience credit for his job. Then he would have had a shorter school day. If he had contacted a family service agency, he might have gotten help with the family situation.

Both of these kids could have been helped with their problems if they had been willing to talk about them. Talking about problems can prevent them from becoming overwhelming.

One girl prevented people from whispering behind her

back about her parents' divorce by telling everyone about it herself. By talking about it openly, she prevented other kids from teasing it out of her. She had no secret for them to find out. The more she talked about it, the more it became a fact of life. She was able to accept it. Since she didn't act ashamed, she didn't encourage kids to treat her as if she had something to be ashamed of. The most shameful events are the ones not talked about; the more they are talked about, the less shameful they seem.

A boy in his last year of high school was so ashamed of his parents' divorce that he asked them not to tell anybody until after he graduated from high school. Keeping the secret became so important that he no longer felt comfortable around his friends. He was so busy not talking to them about the divorce that he couldn't talk to them easily about anything. He tried to keep the secret because he was afraid of losing his friends. Now he was losing his friends by trying to keep the secret. Telling them about the divorce would have been a risk. They might have decided not to speak to him any more. But not telling them about the divorce made him a sure loser.

Some kids can't stand other people knowing about their parents' divorce because if other people know then it will be true. As long as it's a secret, these kids feel there's a chance that their parents may get back together again. Even if they don't know it, they're still dreaming of a reunited family.

In order to settle down into your own life, you have to accept the fact that the divorce is final, that your parents' marriage is over, and that there's nothing you can do to bring them back together.

If you can't get rid of the dream of getting your parents

back together again, you will have trouble settling down into your own life. Even if you have managed on your own through the marriage troubles, separation and divorce, you may need help at this stage to get rid of the dream that is holding you back.

# 13

## Your Own Life

Mark studied the rack of cards carefully. He knew Rachel expected a Valentine, but none of them seemed exactly right for what he was feeling. He didn't want to send her anything too mushy or sentimental. He didn't want it to say too much. He wasn't sure how much he meant to say. Humor didn't seem right either. What he wanted was something direct and on target, without fancy words. But he didn't know what the target was. Did he want to say thanks for their two years together or did he want to say he was finally ready to give her the marriage and baby she had been asking for?

What he wanted to say was: "I want you, but I'm not sure I want to marry you or anybody. I'm not sure what marriage is or means. I'm not sure whether I could make anybody a good husband or whether you or any woman could love me enough to make me a good wife. I think I love you, Rachel, but I distrust love. Will you be my Valentine?''

Mark had an ideal image of what marriage should be. He thought that a married person should feel as warm and close as a baby in its mother's arms. But each partner in a marriage should give the closeness and warmth, and each should receive it. He added to this picture from watching his grandparents and his friends' parents, and from hearing fairy tales. Later on, books he read and movie and television programs he saw built up the fantasy still further.

Mark's own parents had battled silently for years. He remembered the uncomfortable meals, the evenings without a word exchanged between his father and mother. He remembered feeling caught between them in their silent battle. He couldn't help comparing their bitterness to the loving warmth of his ideal image and that comparison still hurt. He wondered how it would be for him if he ever married. Could he ever have the quiet of peace, or would silence always mean hatred for him?

When Rachel brought up the idea of marriage, Mark's old conflict was reawakened. Part of him just said no; he couldn't face that pain again. He had to avoid marriage in order to avoid the painful conflict between his ideal and what he expected the reality to be.

Part of him said yes. He wanted a good marriage. He thought that he had learned what not to do from his parents' mistakes. Now all he needed was to get up the courage to try. Like many adolescents, he had been sure that he didn't want marriage. Now that he was in his twenties, things looked different. He and Rachel had already shared so much; he knew he could count on her to stick by him even when he was between jobs or too sick to be any fun or just plain dull. Marriage was the way to keep her, to make sure she'd always be there for him.

He also wanted to take care of her: The thought that she needed him made him very happy. He loved cooking for her, taking her to football games in the fall, planning vacations for both of them. Marriage would give him the chance to keep all that going forever.

But he was afraid it wouldn't work out that way. People who have been through marriage trouble with their parents are often afraid of becoming dependent on someone else for love. But if they can't overcome their fear, then they certainly will never get what they so much want. Mark was afraid of being dependent on Rachel for love. He was also afraid of Rachel's becoming dependent on him. How could he be responsible for keeping her happy? He thought that if they became dependent on each other, they would only let each other down.

Mark's parents ended their many years of marriage trouble with divorce. Mark had felt abandoned and deserted when his father moved out. He wondered whether there was something wrong with his father. If that were so, maybe he had inherited it or learned it from his father. He worried about this. He also worried that maybe there was something wrong with his mother. Could he have inherited or learned that too? Worst of all was his worry about himself. Maybe his parents had broken up because they couldn't stand living with *him*. Maybe nobody would ever be able to stand living with him.

Even now, as many times as Rachel told him she loved him, he had a hard time believing her. If she loved him, either she couldn't see how worthless he was, or she was willing to settle for a worthless person. He simply couldn't believe that he was lovable.

If he did give in and marry Rachel, he felt sure she would leave him as soon as she found out how worthless he was. The only way to make sure this didn't happen was to keep one eye on the exit door, so that if anybody left, he would be the one.

Mark was also afraid that if he got married, he would lose his crowd of single friends. Then, when Rachel left him, which he was sure would happen eventually, he would have nobody.

This Valentine's Day brought all Mark's wishes and fears to the surface. Like many people, he became especially anxious at holiday times. Such people expect a lot of themselves and others. They expect so much that they are usually disappointed. Valentine's Day revived Mark's wish for a happy marriage. It hurt so much because he was sure he couldn't have it.

Other people feel the same way about Christmas, Passover, New Year's, and other holidays. Some are aware of their painful feelings, but some just get angry at those closest to them at holiday times and don't know why. They want, as Mark did, to get and to give the gifts and flowers and cards that mean love, but they are frightened by their own need.

Mark had moved out into the world. He had separated himself from his parents. He lived with a roommate in an apartment. He was supporting himself. But he still didn't feel completely separate. Even though he had his own friends and his own hobbies, he worried about whether he would end up like his parents.

People who have lived through their parents' marriage

trouble often are afraid of marriage for themselves. Some of them are afraid they will not be able to fulfill their ideal of the perfect marriage. Some are afraid marriage will not keep them from feeling lonely and unloved. Some are afraid marriage will make them old and unattractive. Some are afraid they will never find the right person to spend their lives with. Others are afraid they aren't manly enough or womanly enough to make a good marriage.

Being the child of divorced or separated parents can make it more difficult to build a good marriage of your own. Divorce and separation, like marriage trouble, strongly affect your view of the opposite sex, of yourself, and of marriage. If you didn't have a relationship with your opposite-sex parent, it may be hard for you to find a partner you will be satisfied with. This is because no real-life person can possibly live up to the idealized image you have of your missing parent.

If your opposite-sex parent isn't around during your growing-up years, it would be worth your while to find someone—a teacher, coach, uncle, aunt, grandparent, or other older person—to fill the empty place in your life. This will give you a real-life person to be close to so that you can know what to expect from someone of the opposite sex and how to behave with that person. Such a relationship will increase your chance of building a good marriage in the future.

Everybody has a fantasy of what the perfect marriage should be. It is what happens at the end of the fairy tale. It is the "happily ever after." What people hope for is that marriage will give them someone to care for, who will always be there for them and will always love them. They dream of never being lonely again.

One girl whose parents were never in the house at the same time dreamed of sitting and reading with her future husband. She had never seen her mother and father do that. But she knew it was what she wanted. A boy whose parents never did anything together dreamed of finding a girl to sail around the world with him. That way he could have all the adventure he wanted and still not be lonely.

Children start out wanting the perfect marriage for their parents. Such a marriage makes them feel protected. They dream of having this for themselves when they grow up. They have a fantasy of two people being together always and an idea that by being together they will make life happy for each other. They want the parents' marriage to be like their fantasy and a model for their own marriage. When parents have marriage trouble, their children are disappointed because the parents' marriage does not live up to their fantasy.

Some kids who have grown up in families with marriage trouble give up on the whole idea of marriage. One girl said, "I want children, but I'd rather not have them than have to get married to get them." She thought all marriages must be as painful as her parents' marriage was. She couldn't face the thought of being deserted over and over again as her mother had been.

Other kids think marriage can work, but not for them. Still others think they might someday get married but that their marriage will be completely different from their parents' marriage. One girl imagined her whole life different from her parents' lives. Her parents had battled constantly, were always short of money because of her father's drinking, and hardly ever showed affection toward each other. She pictured herself as having more money, as living in a house rather than an apartment like her parents', and as always having someone to laugh with and hug.

Another girl felt very lonely all the time. Her father was always away on business trips and her mother kept herself from feeling too lonely by going to health spas. The house was almost always empty. The girl pictured herself as the mother of many children in a house in the country that would never be too quiet.

People who have grown up in families with marriage trouble often put off their own marriages because they are afraid the same thing will happen to them.

One girl whose parents had constant battles watched her mother grow fatter and fatter. Her parents would fight. Her mother would sit home and comfort herself with coffee and cake, while her father stormed out. The girl thought her mother had ruined the marriage by getting so fat that her husband didn't want anything to do with her. She thought her mother should be ideally slim, like the models in magazines.

When that girl grew up, she watched her diet very carefully. She enjoyed being slim. She was afraid to marry because she expected marriage to turn her into a saggy, fat, old lady like her mother. She had a secret fear that she would respond to any troubles in her own marriage by overeating also. For her, being single was the guarantee of attractiveness. She stayed model-slim, and she never married. She enjoyed her career and had a full, satisfying life without marriage.

People who grew up hearing their parents arguing over who should do what in the family are often afraid of marriage. They are not sure what is expected of a husband or a wife.

One boy's father refused to do any cleaning inside the house. He would do outside jobs or take out the garbage, but he wouldn't do what he called "woman's work." The boy felt angry at him and sorry for his mother, who had to do all the housework after coming home from her job.

As an adult he had to get over his idea that doing housework would make him less of a man. Until he did he couldn't be a good husband for the kind of independent woman he was attracted to.

One girl often had to take charge of her younger brothers when her parents were too involved in quarreling to notice whether the kids were going to bed. She worried about becoming too bossy, too quick to take charge and make decisions. She thought she would become unwomanly. She wished she could be as passive as her mother. But then who would take care of the boys? She was afraid to marry because she thought no man would ever be able to put up with her bossy ways. She put off marriage until she was thirty. By then she had discovered that men liked her the way she was. She married a man who liked being taken care of the way she had taken care of her brothers.

Some people whose families had marriage trouble feel that marriage would be very good if it worked but terrible if it didn't. They think it is safer not to get too involved with any one person so they can't be hurt by that person. They would rather be moderately comfortable and alone than live in terror of being let down.

One girl decided to be a dancer. She felt she could put off marriage until after she'd had her career. She said, "In dancing, you just have to be good. In marriage you not only have to be good, but you also have to find someone else who's good." She felt she could trust her whole dance company and the orchestra to back her up, but she couldn't trust one person, who might be moody or unreliable, the way she would have to in a marriage.

The most unreliable thing a partner can do is leave the marriage. People whose parents separated or divorced often feel certain that the same thing will happen to them. If your parents separate or divorce, you might think that your own marriage will end the same way. You might think that you have inherited or learned ways of acting from your parents that would make it impossible for you to be a good marriage partner.

A woman whose father had deserted her mother and the children was sure that her future husband would do the same thing. She constantly teased her fiancé about how many other men were interested in her. She felt that she was letting him know how attractive and valuable she was. She was trying to make him jealous. What she didn't know was that he would find the jealousy so painful that he would leave her altogether. What she did made her worst fear come true.

A man whose mother ran away from her husband and children was convinced that women couldn't be trusted. He never was able to trust a woman enough to develop a loving relationship with one. He never married, and although he wanted very much to have children, he had to do without any of his own. But he did become an elementary school teacher and satisfied his need for children that way.

After a divorce some kids lose all contact with one of their parents. One boy was raised entirely by his mother after his father had deserted the family when the boy was five. The boy thought he had picked up ''women's ways'' from being around his mother and her friends so much. He was afraid that he wasn't really manly. He was so afraid of this that he kept having to prove his manhood by having sex with one woman after another. As a man he would have liked to marry, but he couldn't until he got therapy. The therapy helped him change the behavior that was based on old fears.

A girl who lived with her mother after her parents' divorce often heard her mother say, ''All men are alike. They'll cheat on you the minute you take your eyes off them.'' The girl believed her. She never trusted either men or marriage and so she never married.

A boy hearing his mother say the same thing might decide that women were distrustful and would gossip behind his back. He might even get the idea that a real man is supposed to cheat on his wife. That would certainly make it difficult for him to build a good marriage.

Being the child of divorced or separated parents can make it more difficult to establish a good marriage of your own. Divorce and separation, like marriage trouble, strongly affect your view of the opposite sex, of yourself, and of marriage.

If your parents are having marriage trouble or have already separated or divorced, you may wonder whether you will be able to build a good marriage yourself. You can be sure that the experience of your parents' marriage will have affected you and you can expect that the thought of marriage will raise more anxiety in you than in most other people.

This anxiety is both good and bad. It is good because it alerts you to the possibility that things may go wrong so that you can protect yourself from being taken by surprise. If a man had seen his parents' marriage end because they didn't spend enough time talking to each other, he would not be surprised by his wife's complaints that he didn't talk to her.

The anxiety is also good because it allows you to choose your actions by imagining ahead of time what can happen. If a woman had seen her father go out and get drunk whenever her mother yelled at him, she would know that yelling at her own husband might drive him out also, so she would try to express anger without yelling.

Some kids use their parents' marriage failures to help them to be different. They see what doesn't work in their parents' marriage and try to do the opposite in their own.

A man whose parents had divorced while he was quite young decided that he wanted a warm and loving family more than anything else. He married early. He spent most of his nonworking hours with his wife and children. He got great pleasure out of giving his children what he wished he could have had while he was growing up.

Your anxiety about marriage can also be harmful. It's like taking a test in school or being in a play. A little anxiety is necessary to give you the energy to perform at your best; too much may numb you so you can't perform at all. But until you're ready to get married, you don't have to worry about this. Other experiences may help you overcome your fears.

Marriage trouble between your parents is always painful. The worst of it is it's something that happens to you. You can't really do anything to keep it from happening to you. But this book has tried to give you enough information about what's going on so that you can understand it. By understanding, you can master the experience and turn it from something that can tear you apart to something that challenges you to get your own life together.

You don't have to be married to have a good life. But you can have a good life and a good marriage even if your parents didn't. It's up to you to take charge and make the decisions that will make your life your own.

# IV

## A Guide to Getting Help

# 14

## Getting Help

"I can't sit still in school. Teachers throw the same old bull all the time. The place is driving me crazy."

"All the kids laugh at me. I have no friends."

"There's nothing to do after school. Everybody lives somewhere else. Nobody ever calls me."

"I can't get excited about anything. I'm so bored. There's nothing to do all day."

"I don't see why they make us go to all those dumb classes. At least if I cut I can have a good time with my friends."

*"I can't stand it anymore. Sometimes my mother's up till three o'clock in the morning, hollering and cleaning out closets. Other times I don't see her for days. She'll be sleeping in her room day and night."*

*"My father is beating up my mother. I don't know what to do."*

These are things that kids whose families are troubled say over and over again. You may have heard some of your friends saying these things—and you may have said or felt some of them yourself.

All kids have problems. But when your parents are having marriage trouble or have separated or divorced there are more problems to deal with. And even the usual problems often seem worse.

It doesn't matter so much what your problems are; what really counts is how you handle them. In fact, the more serious the problem is, the more satisfaction you can get out of handling it right. Some problems are the kind you can deal with on your own or with help from your friends. Others are not handled so easily.

You may need more help than friends can give. If you have a quarrel with another person, the first thing to do is talk to that person. If your parents' marriage trouble is disturbing your life, then the first people to talk to about it are your parents. You need to tell them how you feel. Do you feel angry, sad, ashamed, abandoned? You need to tell them what makes you feel that way. Is it their quarreling, their silence, their drinking, their never being home? You need to tell them what you want and listen to them when they tell you what they want. You all need to come to an agreement on what you will do for each other.

One girl's parents quarreled a lot about whether her father was having an affair with his secretary. She couldn't stand the arguments. She told her parents that she would drive downtown to pick up her father after work so that her mother could be sure he was coming straight home after work. Since they couldn't stop quarreling and she couldn't tolerate listening to it, they all agreed that she could leave the house to live in a dormitory at college. They would give up the money and she would give up demanding that they stop quarreling. They felt freer now that they knew she wasn't interfering with their lives. By negotiating with her parents, she got herself out of a situation she couldn't stand.

Not all kids think of negotiating with their parents.

The boy who said "I can't sit still in school" was anxious. He never knew when one of his parents' quarrels would erupt into violence. He was always afraid he would come home and find one or both of them injured or even dead. He was anxious in school, but what he was anxious about had nothing to do with what was going on in school. School bothered him because it kept him away from home. Whenever it was quiet and he had to sit still, he was tense. He had images of his mother drowned in the bathtub and his father lying bloody on the floor.

This boy needed help. After getting thrown out of class for disrupting, the boy was assigned to after-school detention, where he was expected to sit still even longer. When he got thrown out of detention, he was suspended from school. The boy needed the kind of help the school couldn't give him. Now that he was out of school, his parents couldn't ignore his problem. He talked it over with them and the principal. They all decided that he should get treatment. He went to a family service agency and talked to a social worker who decided that it was a family problem and the family should get help together. He also got special treatment for himself. This boy could have saved himself a lot of grief at school if he had talked to his parents to begin with.

Another boy told his parents about his worries. He asked them, "You aren't getting divorced, are you? Why can't you stop fighting?" He told them he couldn't stand living with them like that any more, that it was bothering him in school, and that he wanted them to do something about it. Neither parent wanted to harm him. His threat to run away from home finally moved them to act. They went to their local hospital clinic, where they were referred to a center that could give them couple therapy. Even after going into therapy, they continued to fight, but he no longer felt responsible for them. For this boy, getting help meant getting help for his parents so that his own life could be more comfortable.

The girl who said "All the kids laugh at me. I have no friends" had an alcoholic father. She knew that neighbors and classmates had seen him drink. She thought they were laughing about his behavior. She had heard of Alcoholics Anonymous, looked them up in the phone book and asked them what she could do for her father. They told her she couldn't do anything for him and she shouldn't even try. If he wanted to join A.A., he would have to do it on his own. But they gave her the phone number of Al-Anon, a separate group for the families of alcoholics. A woman there told her about an Alateens meeting in her neighborhood. There she made friends with kids who had the same problem she did. No one laughed at her.

One girl ran away from home because she couldn't stand living with her stepfather. Her mother went to the minister of their church to get help in finding her. He found her by talking to other kids. She was in a safe place, with friends, so he persuaded her mother to let her stay there until she was ready to come in and talk about what was bothering her. She did. When she went to the minister for counseling she told him how helpless she felt because she couldn't get the money for clothes and trips that her friends had. The minister found her a baby-sitting and housekeeping job with a family in the parish. The job solved two problems for her. She was able to go to the other family after school, so she didn't have to spend so much time with her stepfather. And she now had the money she wanted. By going to her minister, she got the practical help that clergymen, who often know most of the people in their congregation, are especially able to give.

The boy who said "There's nothing to do after school. Everybody lives somewhere else" was living in a new apartment with his mother after his parents' divorce. He found a magazine from Parents Without Partners lying around the house. It had an article about International Youth Council, an organization for kids from twelve to seventeen who live in single-parent families. He went to meetings, had a good time there, and made new friends.

The boy who said "I can't get excited about anything. I'm so bored" needed the kind of help he couldn't get from friends. He had given up expecting anything from his parents. He couldn't talk about his troubles with his friends.

School just bored him. His parents finally realized something was wrong when he stayed in bed all day on weekends. They took him to a therapist, who recommended a combination of individual and group therapy. Talking with the therapist, and later with other kids in the group, helped him see how he had been putting other people off and keeping them from giving him any stimulation or satisfaction.

The girl who said "I don't see why they make us go to all those dumb classes" ended up in her guidance counselor's office. She hadn't intended to talk about her family problems, but before she knew it she was pouring out the whole story. Her father's gambling was making their lives miserable. They never had enough money for anything, and bill collectors kept phoning. When he lost at cards he yelled at everybody and was impossible to live with. The guidance counselor told her about Gamateen, a group for kids whose parents have gambling problems. There she was told that she hadn't caused her father's gambling, that she couldn't cure it and that she couldn't control it. She was also helped to stop blaming her mother for her father's gambling.

The boy whose mother was always either up all night or sleeping all day finally walked into the emergency room of a nearby hospital. "I need help," he said. "I think my mother is a drug addict. She takes pills all the time. I'm afraid she may end up killing herself." The boy talked to a psychiatric social worker, who called his mother. When she refused treatment, the social worker offered him treatment for himself. His mother allowed him to go. He got help with his worries about what would happen to him if she did take an overdose, and with his fears that it might have been his fault.

A girl in the same kind of family called the Bureau of

Child Welfare in her city. She said, "I can't stand living at home any longer. My mother is strung out on pills half the time and my father's away on business trips and doesn't want to be bothered. I want to get away from them." The Bureau contacted the Family Crisis Clinic of a large hospital in her area. The clinic sent out a team of social workers to look into what was going on. They found that the situation was as bad as the girl had described it, but decided that it would be better to treat the whole family rather than to send her away from home.

Another girl couldn't talk about her troubles. Neither could her mother. Her mother drank to comfort herself when things got too hard for her. The girl felt lonely and abandoned. The girl began drinking too. No one in her family could give her the understanding she needed. The school psychologist, her mother and the principal of her school decided among them that she would be better off in a residential school and rehabilitation center run by the state. Once there, the girl was able to stop drinking.

The boy who said "My father is beating up my mother" was talking to a policeman. He had run out on the street to find one. The policeman went back to his house with him, broke up the fight between his parents, and arrested his father. The boy's mother was angry, so the boy went to live at his aunt's house. At least he was safe there and he didn't have to see his mother being beaten.

If you are having problems like these, you need to tell other people.

Talking with other people about the problems you're having helps keep you from being overwhelmed and ashamed. Other people can help you judge whether you're coping with those problems reasonably well or not. If you can't talk to your friends about your problems, you need to think through for yourself whether you should look for someone with special training in helping others with their problems.

How can you tell when you need this kind of help? One way is to look at the situation you are in. Do you have at least one person you can talk to freely and whom you trust? If there is no such person, then you will have to look for someone with special training.

If it's important to you that what you talk about be kept confidential, be sure to mention it. Do this beforehand and get the person or group you are confiding in to agree. If they say they can't keep it confidential, then you have to decide which is more important: getting the help or keeping the secret.

Suppose you *have* been talking to someone. You may find that the person is unable to give you as much time as you need. Or the person may not feel able to give you the right kind of help. You will need to look for someone who is able to deal with problems like yours and able to set aside the time.

Another way to decide is by looking at yourself.

Are you working well? For most high school kids, school is their major work. If you are reasonably regular in school attendance, on time and awake in classes, working close to your capacity in most of your courses and generally satisfied with school, then you are working well in school. Are there things you like to do outside of school? You might be so interested in music, for instance, that you spend most of your time practicing and booking performances. This is your work. If you're doing well at it, you're working well.

Are you relating well? Do you get along with your parents, your brothers and sisters, the kids at school and most adults? Do you have at least one close friend? Do you have a wider circle of kids your own age you can spend time with?

If you are not satisfied with how you are working, or how you are getting along with other people, if you feel miserable and have no one around to really talk to, then you can ask for help. A trained person can help you in dealing with your parents' marriage troubles, getting through their divorce and settling down in your own life.

If you decide you want therapy, how do you go about getting it?

First, talk to your parents. They'll probably end up paying for the treatment, so it's best to have them on your side from the start. A therapist will not be able to see you for more than one or two visits without your parents' consent anyway.

Then ask around. Talk to your friends, religious counselors, school counselors, a teacher that you trust, or to any doctor you might know. If there isn't anyone you want to ask, don't give up. You can get help through organizations that are listed in the phone book, or through directories available in most libraries.

If your parents have medical insurance, it probably covers at least some of the cost of therapy. If they have no such insurance and if you know they would not be able to afford private therapy for you, call the nearest hospital and

ask if it has a psychiatric clinic. Then ask if there is a service
for adolescents. If you are really in emotional distress and it
is after 5:00 P.M., go to the emergency room of any hospital
and ask to speak to a social worker or psychiatrist. Either of
them will be able to get you the help you need and may also
be able to get your parents to cooperate.

Perhaps you want therapy but can't get your parents to
agree to it. Then you'll need help convincing them. You can
go to a therapist or a hospital emergency room or a mental
health clinic. Ask the therapist to help you get your parents'
consent. As long as you remain at home, it is against the law
for anyone to treat you without their consent.

If they will consent but won't pay, you may be able to
get care at a clinic. If their income is low, the care will be free
or cost very little. If their income is too high to qualify for
free or low-cost services, you may have to get a part-time job
so you can pay for your treatment yourself.

In the unlikely event that your parents won't consent to
therapy, you may still be able to get it. In some states you can
go to family court and ask to be declared a Person In Need of
Supervision (PINS). The court may send you to an agency
which will provide treatment for you. Such agencies as
Jewish Child Care Agency, Catholic Charities and Federa-
tion of Protestant Philanthropies, as well as state and local
mental health agencies, offer treatment to kids referred by
courts.

But you should think carefully before you take such a
step. If a charge of neglect is brought against parents, the
court may remove minor children from the family home and
place them elsewhere. If you have tried every means of

persuading your parents and they still refuse to let you see a therapist, you will need legal advice.

If you want to stop treatment or change therapists, you should tell your therapist. You may be feeling that way because you are getting to some painful feelings which have to be worked through. Staying with the treatment until you have dealt with these feelings may be necessary. Or you may be ready to move on. If that is the case, the quicker you tell your therapist, the quicker you'll get on the right track.

## Where to Start Looking for a Therapist

Organizations to call:

1. Your local mental health association
2. The outpatient psychiatric clinic of your local hospital, or the nearest branch of the American Psychiatric Association
3. Your city's psychiatric society or
4. Family service agency.

Directories to ask for in your local library:

1. National Register of Health Service Providers in Psychology
2. Directory of Medical Specialists
   *Note:* When you locate a therapist, you and your parents will want to inquire about his or her qualifications, fees and methods of treatment.

Finding the names of therapists is only the beginning. Choosing from among qualified licensed people increases the chance that you will find someone who can help. There is a lot of difference between good therapists and poor ones. Good therapists help; poor ones can do harm. The best protection against being harmed by therapy is to make sure that the person has the qualifications and reputation for helping people with your problem.

Choosing the best therapist for you is a very personal thing. You have to decide whether you can respect and work with that person. If you think you can't, you should try someone else. The therapist who is best for your friend may not be the best for you. You have to judge this for yourself.

Some other information you may want:

1.  To find an Alateen group, call the local Al-Anon Information Service (Intergroup) if you are in or near a large city. If there is nothing like this in your local phone book, write to:

    Al-Anon Family Group Headquarters, Inc.
    P.O. Box 182
    Madison Square Station
    New York, New York, 10010

2.  To locate a Gamateen group, call the Gam-Anon number in your local phone book or write to:

    Gam-Anon Family Groups
    P.O. Box 248
    Glassboro, New Jersey 08028

3. If you would like to belong to the International Youth Council, call the local chapter of Parents Without Partners and ask if they sponsor such a group. If they do not, you may want to get nine other kids and form a group of your own. A person may join if he or she is between the ages of twelve and seventeen and if parents are widowed, divorced, separated or never married. Your parents do not have to be members of PWP for you to belong to IYC. For information on starting a group of your own, write to:

IYC Headquarters
7910 Woodmont Avenue
Suite 1000
Washington, D.C. 20014

4. If you have run away from home and need help getting back home or just want to let your parents know you are okay, there are two national numbers to call:

Peace of Mind
1-800-231-6946

National Runaway Switchboard
1-800-621-4000

Both these groups will respect your wish to have your whereabouts kept confidential even though they will encourage you to get back together with your parents.

5.  If you are a Roman Catholic you may want to get in touch with:

    RENEW
    c/o St. Paul the Apostle Church
    415 West 59th Street
    New York, New York 10019

    This is a support community for divorced Catholics.
    RENEW groups are springing up all over the country. Write to the address above to locate a group in your area. Then call the local group to find out if they have a group for kids or if you can help in starting one.

6.  If someone in your family has been or is in prison, and you are looking for kids who have been through the same thing, get in touch with:

    The Fortune Society
    29 East 22nd Street
    New York, New York 10010

    Tell them what you are trying to find. They may be able to help you.

7.  If you think your wishes have not been considered sufficiently in your parents' divorce or separation proceedings and you cannot get your parents to listen to you, you can write or call the Family Court

in your district. Look in the telephone book under the name of your city or county for a Family Court listing. Ask the Information operator to help you if you have trouble finding it. Address your letter or ask to talk to the presiding judge in Family Court. If he or she is not the right person, you will be directed to the right person. Tell that person exactly what you are unhappy about. There is no guarantee that this will bring about the change you want, but at least you will have a chance at it.

8. If you have legal problems and you don't know where to turn, the best thing to do is ask a relative or other adult to go to a lawyer for you. If you can't do this, then look in the telephone book for Legal Aid Society or Legal Services Corp. They will tell you if you are eligible for help by them. If not, they will direct you to someone who can help.

You may be able to get through a crisis without help, but why should you? Doing it yourself can interfere with your growth and distort your personality. By taking on more responsibility than you are ready for, you use up energies that should be going into normal development. Also, by not getting help when you need it, you can get so wrapped up in your own problems that you drive your friends away because they don't enjoy being around you. When this happens, you become even further involved with your own problems, so that your whole view of the world is distorted.

If you think you might need help, it's worth the time and effort it takes to find the right person or group to help you.

You can get help from friends, relatives, school people, groups of people with special kinds of problems, hospitals, social service agencies, therapists, the police and courts, the clergy, and even your own parents. One way to get help from your parents could be to let them read this book.